THE EARL BISHOP

Stephen Price

© Stephen Price 2011

First published in 2011 by Great Sea, Portstewart.

The moral right of the author has been asserted.

All rights reserved. No part of this publication may be reproduced in any material form without the written permission of the copyright owner, except in accordance with the provisions of the Copyright, Designs and Patents Act 1988. Applications for the copyright owner`s written permission to reproduce any part of this publication should be addressed by email to: greatseabooks@btinternet.com

All photographs are copyright of the holders as stated.

ISBN: 978-0-9567993-0-2

Printed and bound by Zing Design and Print, Loughanhill Industrial Estate, Coleraine, County Londonderry. www.zingdp.com

Cover design by Catherine Watt.

Front cover: The Mussenden Temple, Downhill.   © The National Trust

Rear cover: Frederick Hervey, 4th Earl of Bristol, by Elisabeth Vigee Le Brun, Naples, 1790.   © The National Trust

For Kay and Dave Atherton

Prologue

At the edge of a dramatic coastal cliff in Northern Ireland, at a place called Downhill, perches a little temple. Circular in shape, it has classical features like a domed roof, beautiful Corinthian columns and a Latin inscription around its circumference. Translated, the inscription muses how pleasant it is, when the waves of the great sea are tossed by the wind, to watch the struggles of others from the safety of dry land. If somewhat smug, the thought seems appropriate, for the temple overlooks a vast seascape stretching from Donegal in the east, to the Western Isles of Scotland. When the weather is bad, this can be a wild spot indeed.

The Mussenden Temple is Northern Ireland`s best-loved building, but few know very much about it. Who or what was Mussenden and what is such a refined structure doing in such a precarious position? The brooding presence of a ruined mansion on top of the headland only deepens the mystery. Who would build such a grand house in this windswept place? The locals know Downhill as the Bishop`s Palace, because its builder was indeed a bishop, but a bishop like no other. Nowadays, Downhill is cared for by the National Trust and with a bit of reading, the curious may learn that the mansion was once stuffed with treasures: antique statues and paintings by Raphael, Rembrandt, Rubens, Titian and Tintoretto. Yet nowadays, only bare, broken walls remain.

During his lifetime, Frederick Hervey was called many names: Fred, Pansey, the Bishop of Derry, L`Eveque de Derry, il Vescovo Inglese, the Earl Bishop, Bristol, the 4th Earl of Bristol and 'that wicked prelate' (by no less a personage than King George III). In this account, which is not an academic one, rather an attempt to tell his story in an accessible way, he is simply called Frederick. When using quotes from his time, the original punctuation and spelling have been kept, which can be different from today`s, but more evocative.

The Georgian age

Frederick Hervey was born on the 1st of August 1730, at Ickworth, his grandfather's estate in Suffolk, East Anglia, England. Before we say any more about him, it is worth describing the period and circumstances into which he was born. The Industrial Revolution would begin during his lifetime, but not utterly transform Britain until after his death. In the 18th century, Britain and Ireland were still agrarian economies, so land ownership was the primary basis of wealth and this was concentrated in the hands of a few. The population of Britain was just over one-tenth of what it is today and in Ireland, it was slightly more than half. The Kingdom of Great Britain (England, Scotland and Wales) and the Kingdom Ireland, comprising the entire island, were separate entities. However, although Ireland had its own parliament, it was subject to the British one and the King of Great Britain was also the King of Ireland.

Most people were illiterate and lived in primitive conditions, on or below the breadline. Main roads were muddy lanes and the principal form of transport was the horse, for those who could afford one. Steam power was in its infancy and a wooden Royal Navy sailing ship, with its navigation instruments and cannon, represented the apex of viable technology. Sanitation was poor, medical practices were basic and sometimes downright dangerous. Static electricity had been discovered but had no useful application; fresh piped water was a luxury and homes were heated by wood or coal and lit by candle or oil lamp.

Society was rigidly stratified, with royalty at its pinnacle. From 1714 until 1830, four British kings in succession were called George, hence the Georgian age. Royalty surrounded itself with a tiny, noble elite; for most of the 18th century, the English nobility numbered about 160 titles. Next came the gentry, untitled landowners who without working, could live comfortably from rents. Then came the tenant farmers who paid those rents and below them, a mass of uneducated peasantry. Commercial and artisan classes thrived in most towns, but even big cities were small by today's standards. In 1750, London's population totalled 675,000, although this would quickly increase in second half of the century, when the English capital would overtake Amsterdam as Europe's largest city. There was an explosion in trade as Britain expanded colonially, although the Georgian middle class was modest in size compared to the later Victorian period. It was a time of enlightenment, however the slave trade was still legal and hanging was a common punishment, even for petty crimes committed by children. The British Isles were on the verge of enormous change, but in Frederick's day would still have been more recognisable to an Elizabethan eye, than to a modern one.

Frederick's first stroke of luck was to be born into the elite. If he had been born to a farmer's wife, just outside the gates of Ickworth Park in Horringer village, we would never have heard of him. Even today, Horringer is a quiet hamlet, a few miles from the historic Suffolk town of Bury St Edmunds. The region of East Anglia was England's bread basket and prospered in the pre-industrial era. By 1730, the Herveys had already owned Ickworth for three centuries, but Frederick's grandfather, John Hervey, was a shrewd, godly man who married twice and both times well, adding to his inherited property by acquiring land with each wife. To give some idea of his wealth, at that time the rent from 200 acres was enough to fund a decent lifestyle. John owned 30,000 acres, in Suffolk, Lincolnshire and Essex. Until 1714, he had been a baron, but then was made an earl for backing the right side – that is to say, the winning one – in England's choice of king.

At least he was a Protestant

In matters spiritual, modern England is a tolerant society, however in the 18th century, religion was still a highly contentious issue; not because people were particularly moral or devoted, because compared to the 19th century, generally they weren't. Rather, after 150 years of bloody upheaval, power now rested with adherents of the Protestant faith and they had no intention of relinquishing it. Since Henry VIII's death in 1547, Protestant and Catholic claimants had fought over England's throne in a titanic struggle that had pitted the country against its European neighbours and caused three civil wars, numerous revolts and countless martyrdoms and executions. As recently as 1688, the Dutch Protestant, William of Orange, had overthrown his uncle and father-in-law, the English Catholic King James II, in the Glorious Revolution. Partly played out in Ireland, episodes included the siege of Derry and the Battle of the Boyne, events which still resonate there today.

When William's cousin and successor, Queen Anne of Great Britain, died in 1714, Frederick's grandfather was 49. At least fifty Catholic relatives had a claim to the throne, including Anne's half-brother, the Old Pretender, James Francis Edward Stuart. However, the law decreed (and still does) that a Catholic monarch could not rule Britain, therefore the crown went to her second cousin, Georg Ludwig, the prince-elector of Hanover, in what is now modern Germany. So began the Hanoverian succession. A total stranger to Britain, King George I did not speak English and was more preoccupied with German affairs than British ones, so he was not an overwhelmingly popular choice of sovereign, but at least he was a Protestant.

John Hervey was a staunch Whig, one of the two great British political parties of the period. Whigs advocated a constitutional monarchy – a king chosen by and ruling alongside parliament – whereas Tories believed in the divine and hereditary rights of royalty, which at that time, meant the deposed Stuart family. Only men owning a certain amount of property were allowed to vote, or about five percent of the adult male population. John had always worked hard to return Whig candidates to parliament, including himself, and was vociferous in his support for the new German king. So in November 1714, shortly after his coronation, George I visited John's

London house at 6 St James`s Square and made him the 1st Earl of Bristol.

The Herveys had never been associated with Bristol the city, which is on the other side of England and a good 150 miles from Bury. Yet the apparent link has generated myths like Frederick lending his name to the famous sherry, Harvey`s Bristol Cream, which was in fact christened for an unrelated wine merchant. The nominal connection arose because at the time of John`s elevation, new titles were not being created, so he had to pick from a selection of defunct peerages. The earldom had originated with the Digby family of Dorset, but had lapsed in 1698. John Digby, the 'first' 1st Earl of Bristol, had been a Catholic convert and a royalist, so Hervey saw a poetic justice in the title being assumed by a staunchly Protestant parliamentarian.

Men, Women and Herveys

To reflect his new status, the 1st Earl planned a grand mansion for Ickworth, but it was never built because although he was wealthy on paper, there were many drains on his resources. His second wife, Frederick`s grandmother, Elizabeth Felton, much preferred London court life to sleepy Suffolk. She reputedly had two lovers and, as was then fashionable, gambled and partied heavily, vices that her sons would inherit. So in spite of his financial acumen, thanks to his immediate family, the 1st Earl was often short of money. By the time Frederick was born, he had retired to Ickworth, creating a beautiful parkland by the simple expedient of ordering his tenant farmers to move to Horringer village. His home, Ickworth Lodge, was really a glorified farmhouse, but he was happy there.

Another myth attached to Frederick is that he was born by Caesarean section, which is hard to imagine since at that time, women rarely survived such a drastic operation. Yet Frederick`s mother, Molly Leppell, not only survived his birth but would have more children.

Whatever the case, Frederick was a physically slight baby, which the 1st Earl attributed to Molly indulging in *'dancing, morning suppers, sharp wines, china oranges, &c (etcetera),'* during her pregnancy. Since Molly lived at Ickworth, the old man was in a position to know. Nonetheless, Frederick gained strength and on the 3rd of September 1730, his baptism was attended by three of the most socially fashionable people in the country: the Prince of Wales, the Duke of Richmond and the Duchess of Marlborough. Frederick was even named after the Prince, who was Frederick Louis. However, this illustrious company was not a reflection of the baby`s importance, rather of his father`s.

John Hervey – as the eldest son we can call him Lord Hervey, to distinguish him from the 1st Earl – was a prominent figure at the court of King George II, who had recently succeeded George I. A favourite of Queen Caroline, Lord Hervey was also, like the 1st Earl before him, the Whig member of parliament for Bury. Unlike his father, he was a bisexual and famous for his good looks and wit. He joked about himself that his coat of arms should have been *'a cat scratchant.'* The French philosopher Voltaire, who had visited England in the 1720s and been quite smitten by Molly, is attributed with saying about her husband that: '*When God created the human race, he created men, women and Herveys*' (although the quote is so good that it is claimed by at least three other people, including Lord Hervey`s friend, Lady Mary Wortley Montagu).

Lord Hervey`s sexuality did not prevent him from having female lovers and siring seven siblings for Frederick, but he is mainly remembered today for the venomous satire on his personality by the poet Alexander Pope, who christened him Lord Fanny:

'Amphibious Thing! that acting either Part,
The trifling Head, or the corrupted Heart!
Fop at the Toilet, Flatt`rer at the Board,
Now trips a Lady, and now struts a Lord.'

Pope was a Catholic and a Tory, so opposed Lord Hervey politically. Worse, he had been a friend who through jealousy had turned foe; he had been in love with Molly before she married Hervey. Still, the image of a tricksy, vain bisexual has stuck, partly because it was true. Lord Hervey was not a good husband or father and spent as little time as possible with his wife, parking her at Ickworth whilst he threw himself into London court life. He had no time for his children whatsoever, except (as in the case of Frederick's christening) when he could use them socially.

Molly was a beautiful, educated woman and a former lady-in-waiting herself, but could only languish on the sidelines as Lord Hervey spent most of his spare time with his male lover, Stephen Fox, who was also member of parliament. She was even sometimes reduced to writing to Fox for news of her husband, who, it was rumoured, had also seduced the Prince of Wales. If that was true, it meant that when Frederick was a child, his father had affairs with Stephen Fox, the king's son and a maid of honour called Anne Vane, which was not bad going for a *'Fop at the Toilet.'*

Sodomy was still a capital crime, but amongst the five hundred or so people who made up Britain's ruling class, Lord Hervey's antics were more a source of gossip than of scandal. The normal rules generally did not apply to the aristocracy and this was a morally ambivalent age. Even so, when Frederick was five months old, Lord Hervey fought a sword duel with another friend turned foe, William Pulteney (later the 1st Earl of Bath), who had publicly accused him of homosexuality. Both men walked away, aptly enough, with scratches.

None of this could have impacted on the baby Frederick. Indeed, shortly after his baptism, his parents left him with his grandparents at Ickworth and went to London, Lord Hervey to return to court and Molly for a rare treat.

If you call a dog Hervey

Frederick was no doubt fondly received, but he was a third son and a fifth grandchild, so in the grand scheme of things was merely another addition to the Hervey brood. The law of male primogeniture meant that first-born sons were automatic heirs, so quite a few potential candidates stood before Frederick in the queue for his grandfather`s fortune and titles; his own father; his eldest brother, George, and any legitimate son he might have; then his second oldest brother, Augustus, and any legitimate son he might have. So Frederick`s childhood was little commented upon, but a fair portion of it was spent at Ickworth, because the 1st Earl doted on his grandchildren, even though their grandmother hated having them around and referred to them as *'young vermin.'*

The Herveys had served the English crown as far back as Henry VIII, which considering how often and bloodily it had changed hands over the centuries, showed remarkable tact and guile. However, with the arrival of Elizabeth Felton, the family lost its reputation for boring reliability and instead became known for its barking eccentricity. Frederick`s grandmother hailed from Playford Hall near Ipswich, a moated manor house which still partly stands today. Like Frederick`s mother, she too had been a lady-in-waiting and along with her fondness for the party lifestyle, she brought a mad streak to the Herveys, as well as predispositions towards both gout and epilepsy.

Lord Hervey inherited her epilepsy. Her gout (or more correctly, the wide range of complaints then collectively called gout) would afflict most of her grandsons. With age also came instability; even Lord Hervey, who abandoned poor Molly to her tender mercies at Ickworth, compared his mother`s mouth to the crater of Vesuvius: *'Everything that comes out of it that is not fire, is rubbish; everything that is within reach of its disagreeable influence is the worse for it.'*

Lord Hervey was quite a character, but his younger brothers – Frederick`s uncles – were just as colourful. Tom eloped with his godfather's wife then hurled abuse at his friends and family through a series of raving pamphlets. Harry was a youthful tearaway who joined the army and was rarely out of trouble, but then sobered up for long enough to marry an heiress, change his name to Hervey-Aston and become a clergyman. Nonetheless, when the famous writer, Samuel Johnson, first came to London as a penniless student, both Tom and Harry looked after him. Johnson later said of Harry: *'he was a vicious man, but very kind to me; if you call a dog Hervey, I shall love him.'* Another uncle, a Royal Navy captain called William, was so vicious that he was court-martialled out of the service; an extraordinary achievement, given the Georgian Navy's reputation for brutality. So no doubt it was a relief, to his mother at least, that by the time he reached school age, Frederick had developed into a calm, intelligent child.

A model student

When he was 6 years old, Frederick was sent to Doctor Newcomb's school in Hackney, which was then a village on the north-eastern outskirts of London. Doctor Newcomb educated many of the sons of the great and the good. When Frederick turned 11, he progressed to Westminster School, where the children of the great and the good are educated to this day. He was diligent and well-liked and some of his contemporaries would remain friends for life. One in particular, William Hamilton, is worth mentioning now, for the influential role he would later play.

When Frederick was 13, his father died, a lonely and broken man. Lord Hervey's stellar success at court had dissolved into bitter failure. He had made too many enemies and had lost his looks, health and lovers, both male and female. He died aged 47 and in debt, leaving nothing to Molly, but £100 per year to Frederick. Depending on how it is calculated, the value of money varies wildly across the centuries, but measured against the retail price index, £100 then would be worth approximately £16,000 today. For a more helpful comparison, one might consider that at the time, a fully-employed agricultural labourer could have expected to earn £15 per year, so £100 probably seems a tidy enough sum for a student to be getting by on. For a nobleman`s son, it was a pittance, and because of his father`s indebtedness, Frederick may not have received all the money anyway. It was one thing to settle an allowance on someone and quite another for that allowance to be paid.

Westminster School has always prided itself on turning out independent thinkers, an ethos which worked in Frederick`s case. The 18th century was also the neoclassical age, when the philosophy, art and literature of ancient Greece and Rome were back in vogue. After more than a millennium of being forgotten or ignored, the archaeological remains of the classical world were being excavated by enthusiastic amateurs all over the Mediterranean. It was fashionable for English aristocrats to travel there on the Grand Tour, and view these wonders for themselves. Rome had a permanent English artistic community and the designs of the Italian Renaissance architect, Andrea Palladio, were all the rage. These were copied and adapted in the fine mansions that sprang up all over Britain and Ireland, built by landowners keen to flaunt their wealth and sophistication. The very word 'classical' comes from the Latin for 'belonging to the highest class of citizens,' and the European aristocracy of the 18th century saw itself as no less than a second flowering of this golden age – hence 'neoclassical,' or 'new classical.'

This exalted self-image accompanied an automatic sense of entitlement to incredible wealth and privilege, but it also indicated a growing intellectual enlightenment. For a person of taste, reason became the guiding force, as opposed to superstition or religion. Besides appreciating art and literature, educated noblemen were expected to pursue a scientific interest, no matter how erratically. Europe`s colonial powers were exploring, mapping and fighting over a still largely-unknown world; Frederick was educated two decades before Captain Cook`s first great Pacific voyage. Although books were luxury items, the period saw the rise of a new literary form, the novel. Ideas spread quickly through pamphlets, tracts and journals, cheaply produced by the printing press. Philosophers like John Locke and Voltaire had elevated the experience of being human and questioned religious dogma, whilst the liberal romanticism of Jean-Jacques Rousseau encouraged men and women to raise their emotions to new heights. Feelings were good, and the more effusively-expressed, the better.

In this heady atmosphere, Frederick next went up to Cambridge, where he was accepted into Corpus Christi, then known as Benet College. Benet was noted for producing great antiquarians and Frederick was described by a fellow-student thus: *'his good sense, great good nature and affability gained him the love and esteem of all who knew him; as his sprightliness, wit, vivacity, ingenuity and learning proved him to be a genuine Hervey.'* Since nobles were entitled to a degree without taking examinations, such model behaviour was not necessarily the norm.

Career opportunities

For a young man in Frederick`s situation, from a titled family but with little chance of inheriting, career choices were limited to the army, the navy, the church or the law. All the top positions in these branches of state were in the gift of parliament and the king. Society functioned through what we would now deem a corrupt and shamelessly nepotistic system of patronage. Such practices have not been eradicated today, but where they do exist in developed countries, are hidden and frowned upon when uncovered. In the Georgian era, powerful, well-paid jobs were openly given in exchange for political support and it was entirely expected that the incumbents would then fill every post beneath them with relatives, friends, sons of friends and stooges. Getting on life was all about connections and for every salaried position that fell vacant, a pile of petitions would land on the patron`s desk. Even when positions did not fall vacant, petitions arrived anyway, showering the patron with flattery and reminding them what a loyal servant they would have, if they could see their way to employing the petitioner`s talents at the next available opportunity. Today, we would use the term 'canvassing.'

For example, at the tender age of 11, Frederick`s older brother, Augustus, had gone to sea as a cabin boy on his uncle William`s ship, the *Pembroke*. Since this was the same uncle who was too much of a disciplinarian even by naval standards, one can just imagine some of the delights that young Augustus was exposed to, but at least he was embarked on a career which, through persistence and yet more patronage, would see him a Vice-Admiral in his early fifties.

After Frederick`s father died, his eldest brother, George, became heir presumptive to the 1st Earl`s estates, who was still at that point enjoying a long and happy retirement. Spoiled, fractious and unhealthy like his grandmother, George fought often with his mother, Molly. Her favourite son was Augustus and she must have pined terribly during his early years at sea. However, after her husband`s death, she was able to live more on her own terms. She stayed on at Ickworth but also rented a small, beautifully-decorated house near St James`s Park in London, where she became mistress of her own social salon. She was a cosmopolitan lady; regular guests included noted liberals and many Catholics, with whom she was openly friendly.

Frederick, having inherited his mother`s cultured and tolerant disposition, chose not to submit himself to the hardships of a military existence. So in 1748, at the age of 18, he opted for the law, and was accepted into Lincoln`s Inn. This meant moving to Holborn in London and effectively joining a large bachelor community. There, he laboured away for three years, until his grandfather died in 1751, at the impressive old age of 86, which was more than double the average life expectancy of the time. Unlike Frederick`s father, the 1st Earl had shepherded his fortune, recovering from the profligacy of his nearest and dearest. All his land, money and titles passed to Frederick's eldest brother, George, who now became the 2nd Earl of Bristol. This was a spot of good news for Frederick, because benevolent as the old man had been, he had also become careful of his purse, whereas George was more casually generous (to Frederick, at least). Rather than follow a predictable path, it was also around this time that Frederick showed the first signs of doing as he pleased with his life, when he threw himself into a forbidden romance.

Frederick the lover

The Herveys were the great Whig family of Bury St Edmunds. Their arch-rivals, the Davers family, were Tories. The Davers family seat was a magnificent moated Tudor mansion called Rushbrooke Hall, which until it was demolished in 1961, stood as the crow flies less than five miles from Ickworth. Sir Jermyn Davers had often competed with Frederick's grandfather to buy the votes of the good burghers of Bury and when he had died in 1742, his wife, Lady Davers, had continued to oppose the Herveys with great vigour. She had originally been a parson's daughter and oddly for that time, she and Sir Jermyn had lived openly together for ten years, even producing children, before they had finally married. Lady Davers was a formidable woman. She had a daughter called Elizabeth, who was three years younger than Frederick. A sensible, well-educated girl, Elizabeth was handsome, rather than pretty. Frederick called her 'Excellent'. She was 19, he was 22, and both families opposed their relationship. So without approval, the young couple married on the 10th of August 1752, in Rushbrooke church, which still stands to this day. Although her own marital history was hardly exemplary, Lady Davers refused to speak to Elizabeth for over a year. The matriarch's overbearing character was partly blamed for the strange melancholy that afflicted Elizabeth's brothers, two of whom would go on to shoot themselves, one in his mother's greenhouse and the other out at sea. A third wandered deep into the wilds of North America, where he was killed by the natives near Lake Huron.

Fortunately, Elizabeth was a more stable type. She brought a small dowry of £3,000 and the young couple spent their first few months of married life avoiding Bury, meandering between London and the village of Alwalton, near Peterborough. Their first child, Mary, arrived in the spring of 1753. The exact date and location of Mary`s birth appear to have been lost, which could suggest that Elizabeth might have been pregnant when she married. Whether that is an unfair assumption, it soon ceased to matter, for by the autumn, the dust had settled sufficiently for the little family to return to Bury, where they took a small house in the town. Frederick complained of the rent – forty guineas – and worried about not being able to afford furniture, which shows that for young, married couples, some things have not changed.

Frederick still travelled to London for his legal studies, but stayed less at Lincoln`s Inn and more at 6 St James`s Square, now his brother`s townhouse. During a visit there, he met his younger sister, Mary, who was on the run from her husband in Ireland, a rascally squire called George Fitzgerald, of Turlough, County Mayo. This encounter is worth noting because Mary was the first Hervey to live in Ireland and her even more rascally son, George Robert, 'the Fighting Fitzgerald', would later feature in Frederick`s life in a way that no-one could then have foreseen.

Frederick the clergyman

In another sign that he intended to follow his own star, Frederick quit the law. As one contemporary remarked: *'his parts were too lively for the plodding gravity of that profession.'* Frederick had a younger brother called William, who for most of his teens had intended to become a clergyman, but in 1754 changed his mind and decided to join the army. That summer, Frederick wrote to a relative:

'In consequence of this step of William's, & since he has resolv'd not to be a Clergyman I think I have determin'd to become one – my Inclination, my interest, and tho' last mention'd yet first consider'd, Mrs. Hervey's desire, all unite and have all been strengthen'd by my brother's approbation, so that nothing now remains to complete my scheme, but some preparation and the due time to execute it.'

So a combination of family circumstances – his younger brother's change of heart, Elizabeth's wishes and the 2nd Earl's approval – led Frederick to the church. God did not come into it. Indeed, during his long ecclesiastical career, doubt was expressed by many people in many countries that Frederick believed in God at all. However, his intelligence and learning would allow him to move in religious circles with ease. At best, he seems to have been a Deist, perhaps vaguely acknowledging a divine but indifferent Creator who did not intervene in human affairs. As his story unfolds, we shall most definitely see that his approach to religion was ecumenical, in that he did not uphold the merits of one faith over another. It must also be remembered that thanks to his classical education, Frederick would have been as familiar with the deeds of Zeus as those of Jesus and would have appreciated a painting of Venus as readily as one of the Virgin Mary. His letters from the time show no preoccupation with religious matters, much less a zealous awakening of the Christian spirit. Rather, the life of a clergyman would be *'easier to pursue.'* In this sense, he was no different from hundreds of other minor nobles who joined the church purely for an income. The practice was so common that it gave rise to a lower rung of pastoral shepherd; curates, paid by the established clergy to do their duties for them.

Frederick took his degree from Cambridge without sitting examinations and was made a deacon by the Bishop of Ely in August 1754. He was ordained a priest the following January and moved his family into a modest cottage on the edge of the Ickworth estate, loaned by brother George. He did not bother with any parochial work, rather he and Elizabeth got down to the more pleasurable if less saintly business of making babies. The couple's first son, named for brother George, was born that October; then another boy, John Augustus (or Jack as he was more commonly called), on New Year's Day 1757. A sister for Mary, Elizabeth Christina, came in the spring of 1758; her pet name was Bess. A third son died in infancy in 1761.

With all these mouths to feed, money – or the lack of it – was never far from Frederick's mind. He dedicated himself to chasing 'preferments,' petitioning powerful patrons for better-paid posts. So eagerly did he undertake this task, that on one occasion in July 1760, he petitioned the Duke of Newcastle for the Deanery of Bristol, which was in that noble's gift. Frederick had heard that the incumbent had died, so he offered the Duke his condolences and himself as the ideal replacement. One can imagine his horror when the Duke replied:

'Sir,
I recd. the favour of your letter and believe and indeed hope that you are misinformed with relation to the vacancy of the Deanery of Bristol. My friend Dr Squire, Dean of Bristol was in extreme good health on Friday last, and I have heard nothing to the contrary since; and I observe that your letter was dated from Ickworth Lodge that day.'

Frederick's response was a masterpiece of grovelling, but this setback did not stop him from pestering every person of influence he knew. His persistence bore some fruit; before he died, his father had briefly held the honorary civil post of Lord of the Privy Seal, so probably for that reason, in 1756 Frederick was given the much less lucrative position of Clerk of the Privy Seal. In 1763, he was made Chaplain to King George III, a more prestigious job title but again, not very well paid. Either his duties were very light or he ignored them, because two years later, he was able to embark with his family on the first of his epic trips abroad.

Frederick the traveller

It may seem odd that a rural clergyman with financial worries would even contemplate a prolonged continental holiday, especially accompanied by his wife and children, but in fact Frederick had a money-saving motive. Since the 1750s, British tourism abroad had dried up because of the Seven Years`War. The first 'global' conflict had started between Britain and France over their North American colonies, then spread to Europe with Prussia on Britain`s side and Austria, Russia and Sweden backing France. Now the war was over and it was safe to cross the English channel again. Since the cost of living was lower in most continental countries, it made financial sense to spend time there and many English aristocrats nurtured their money in this manner. Mary and Bess, who were now 12 and 7 years old, were to join a boarding school in Geneva – a further saving. George, then aged 9, would accompany his parents whereas Jack, then 8, would stay behind in Bury.

Health was another motive for travel. Not only was its climate warmer, but the continent was dotted with spa towns, where the waters were deemed a cure for many ailments. Finally, there was the not-insignificant matter of the Grand Tour, that aristocratic rite of passage which until now, had eluded Frederick. Being able to discuss first-hand the art, architecture, manners and music of mainland Europe added that final touch of polish to a person of Frederick`s class and since nobility across the continent shared similar educational and cultural values, one could network socially. As well as saving money, Frederick was keen to meet people and to see the sights.

However, what started as a wonderful adventure soon took a terrible turn, when after a sojourn in Paris, young George died in the Belgian town of Spa. Ironically, the Herveys were there to avail of the invigorating hot springs. It is not known what George died of, but since no accident is mentioned, presumably he succumbed to an illness. By modern standards, child mortality rates were high and even a healthy adult could be abruptly dispatched by any one of a number of diseases, some of which have since been eradicated. Frederick and Elizabeth were devastated; even years later, Frederick could not mention George without being overcome by emotion.

Nowadays, parents in such tragic circumstances would immediately return home, but the loss did not prevent the Herveys from travelling on to Geneva and depositing Mary and Bess, as planned, at the school of a Mademoiselle Chomel. However, it must be wondered whether the eventual disintegration of this affectionate family might have had its genesis in this trip. Although she would remain a loyal wife for many years to come, Elizabeth Hervey grew to loathe travelling as much as her husband loved it. After Switzerland, her letters show how much she missed her daughters and the dreadful thought must have occurred to her that if only she had stayed in England, she might still have had all her children around her, including poor George.

Before moving on to Italy, the couple visited Voltaire, who had known Frederick`s parents (and had particularly admired his mother). The great philosopher had established himself just across the French border with Switzerland in the town of Ferney, where he had built a church and a theatre. Pointing them out to Frederick, he asked in which building the biggest farce was played. Frederick had sufficiently recovered his sense of humour to reply: *'That depends entirely upon the author.'* Elizabeth, on the other hand, disliked Voltaire; when he died thirteen years later, she called him *'wretched.'*

Vases and volcanoes

In the mid-18th century, the map of mainland Europe was quite different from the one we know today. Spain, Portugal and France were recognisable, but where one would expect to find Germany and Italy, instead there existed a complicated patchwork of smaller states, electorates and principalities. Germany was still known as the Holy Roman Empire, although confusingly its borders lay very far from Rome. The Eternal City was part of the Papal States and Naples was the capital of its own kingdom, covering the southern half of the Italian peninsula. For the sake of convenience, we will still refer to Germany and Italy, but is worth bearing in mind that each separate statelet had its own rulers, laws and currency. This made travel a slow affair, never mind the appalling roads. However, people were in less of a rush and often happy to linger in one place for weeks or even months, before moving onto the next.

By early 1766, Frederick and Elizabeth had travelled as far south as Naples, where Frederick's old school chum, William Hamilton, was British ambassador to the Kingdom of the Two Sicilies, as the Neapolitan dominion was then called. Hamilton's first wife, Catherine Barlow, was still alive and like Elizabeth Hervey, was a mild and modest soul. Of Hamilton's rather less modest second wife, we shall hear more later.

Hamilton's diplomatic duties mainly involved socialising and keeping a weather eye on the court of the King Ferdinand I, which was not a demanding task since the Neapolitan monarch was notoriously lazy. So the Englishman had plenty of time to engage in the two pursuits that intrigued him the most; collecting vases and studying volcanoes. Hamilton was an expert antiquarian and to supplement his diplomatic income, he dealt in artefacts, buying them cheaply as they were dug from the ground and selling them to touring nobility. Part of his personal collection of Greek vases forms the foundation of the antiquities section of the British Museum. The artefacts came from tombs dotted around the countryside, plundered now after many centuries to feed the burgeoning demand for all things classical. Hamilton had another source; the towns and villas that had been buried by the eruption of Vesuvius in 79 AD, including Pompeii, which had only recently been rediscovered. Vesuvius dominates the Bay of Naples and is still active. In 1766, it put on quite a display for the visiting Herveys, spitting rock and fire from its cone.

It has already been noted that the enlightened nobleman pursued the sciences as well as the arts, since the two disciplines were not as specialised as they are today. Through his host, Frederick now acquired two of the grand obsessions that would dominate his life; vulcanology – the study of volcanoes – and collecting antiquities. Since he was still a man of modest means, he was more able to indulge the former, but his new fascination was almost snuffed out just as soon as it started. That April, in a letter to his eldest daughter, Mary, at her boarding school in Geneva (in which he scolds her for her spelling in her letters to him – she was still only 13), Frederick describes an ascent of Vesuvius:

'After about an hour's fatigue we reach'd the summit, where we found a great hollow of about forty feet & half a mile round: at the bottom of this were two large mouths from whence the mountain frequently threw up two or three hundred red hot stones some as big as your head, and some considerably larger; one of these struck me on the right arm, and without giving me much pain at the time made a wound about 2 inches deep, tore my coat all to shreds, & by a great effusion of blood alarm'd my companions more than myself. In a few days it became very painfull, then dangerous, and so continued to confine me to my bed & room for near five weeks.'

If that stone had fallen six inches to the left, our story would have ended here. Whatever alarm her father's letter must have caused, poor Mary must have felt a different sort of sympathy for her mother, because her letters were almost entirely preoccupied with the rigours of travel; dirty beds, ill-tempered drivers and even a frightening night abandoned alone by the roadside, somewhere near Monte Cassino.

A Corsican hero

Frederick was not, at this time, neglectful of Elizabeth. The incident near Monte Cassino had been a traveller`s accident; he had galloped ahead to find a bed for the night and become lost, then Elizabeth`s carriage had become stuck. Nonetheless, he was in the habit of depositing her for weeks at a time while he went off and did his own thing. No doubt, she was glad of the break. Having lived an uneventful life until his mid-thirties, Frederick`s newfound passion for volcanoes perhaps betrayed an awakening side of his character that thrived on drama – danger, even. A diversion he made at this point fits the emerging pattern; in the summer of 1766, he left Elizabeth on the Italian mainland and sailed for Corsica, to meet a freedom fighter.

Just five years older than Frederick, the Corsican patriot Pasquale Paoli had already spent a decade resisting the French and the Genovese, who had occupied his native island. Anyone who antagonised the French was usually a hero to the English and it also helped that Paoli was ruggedly handsome and classically-educated. In 1766, he had fought his enemies to a temporary stalemate, although he would eventually lose his struggle and spend long epsiodes of exile in London.

By the expedient of lashing his carriage to the mast and not stepping out of it, Frederick made the sea crossing to Corsica, where he was entertained by the French. Then he crossed no-man`s land to the spectacular hilltop town of Corte, to meet Paoli himself. The great liberator hosted Frederick for over a week, during which time he imagined himself *transported 2,000 years back to the ages of Grecian heroism.* On the return voyage, Frederick`s ship was pursued by Turkish pirates, but he made it safely to the mainland; not a bad adventure for a rural English clergyman. The romantic image of a dashing yet noble freedom fighter must have impressed Frederick, for he would recreate it years later in a country which, at the age of 36, he had yet to visit, but would soon come to know well.

Family connections

Brother George, the 2nd Earl, was a pompous hypochondriac who, fearing attacks of the gout, lived mostly off boiled vegetables and milk. However, he had once challenged a man to a duel for spitting in his hat. More gratifyingly, in 1755 he had been appointed British ambassador to the court of Turin (then capital of the independent Duchy of Savoy) and in 1757 became ambassador to Madrid, which was an important post. Although George was generous, because of his frail constitution he had always sought positions in warm countries, which was nice for him but not much use to a younger brother, itching to exploit his connections.

Then in 1766, the Whig statesman William Pitt the Elder became the political leader of Britain for the second time. George was considered to have done a good job in Madrid and was reliably Whiggish, so that August, Pitt appointed him Viceroy of Ireland. The viceroy, or Lord Lieutenant, was the king`s representative and Ireland`s most powerful individual, dispensing patronage and generally ensuring that in all important matters, Britain`s will would be done. Pitt wanted George to keep the Irish parliament under control whilst attempting to improve the lot of the Irish Catholics, most of whom lived in shocking poverty.

This was a tall order, for although Ireland was enjoying a period of relative peace, appearances could be deceptive. Since the early decades of the century, Irish Catholics had been subject to the Penal Laws, which prevented them from voting, entering politics, buying land, receiving a decent education, practicing law, joining the army, or owning a weapon. This created no small degree of resentment, a feeling shared by Presbyterians, who, as dissenters from the established church, were subject to many of the same restrictions. The only worthwhile avenue left open to adherents of oppressed religions was trade, which had created middle-class minorities with enough cohesion to start making their grievances heard. However, the Irish parliament gave no succour to the disaffected, since it was the plaything of Ireland's landowning class, the Protestant Ascendancy. In turn, the Irish parliament was subjugated to the British one and could not pass laws without its permission.

In every corner of the world, the long-term strategy of British colonialism was that of divide and rule; to set the natives fighting amongst themselves, usually along religious or ethnic grounds, then to govern through a small ruling class. Thus, vast tracts of territory could be exploited with relatively little manpower. As England's oldest overseas colony, the method had been perfected in Ireland and its repercussions are still evident to this day. In the 18th century, although Catholics comprised three-quarters of Ireland's population of 3.5 million people, they had little or no power and owned just one-twentieth of the land. Numerically, the remaining quarter of the population was divided between around 600,000 Presbyterians, who were mainly the descendants of Scottish settlers and concentrated in the north, and 400,000 Protestants, who formed the ruling minority.

At the time of brother George's appointment, Ireland's different factions did have one complaint in common; England's restrictions on trade. The British parliament had banned the export of Irish wool, a commodity that the country was particularly good at producing. Alcohol, linen, glass and iron manufacture were similarly banned or taxed, to thwart competition for British producers. In 1740-1, Ireland had suffered a terrible famine, but had now recovered to the point where it was ready to flourish economically. To further that aim, the Irish parliament wanted legal parity with the British one.

The personal solution devised by brother George to govern this powderkeg was to never set foot in Ireland at all. Pitt fell ill and within six months, George resigned his commission, although he kept his salary and the £3,000 Pitt had given him for relocation expenses to Dublin. He also wasted no time in dispensing patronage. As viceroy, he could appoint bishops to the Church of Ireland, the established equivalent of the Church of England. Britain's first minister and the king usually rubber-stamped such recommendations and Derry, the richest bishopric in the country, was expected to fall vacant at any moment, owing to the ill-health of the incumbent, a Dr. William Barnard. However, Dr. Barnard did not oblige the Herveys by dying at this exact moment in time and the first see to fall vacant under George`s tenure was a small one at the opposite end of the island; Cloyne, not far from the city of Cork.

A Cork Bishop

Frederick was somewhere en route from Venice to Geneva when he heard the good news. The king himself, now George III, had warmly approved Frederick`s appointment to Cloyne. The Herveys picked up Mary and Bess from their boarding school and headed for London via Paris, where Frederick was entrusted with a secret letter from the ambassador, for Pitt`s eyes only. He would grow to love this sort of intrigue and was already an admirer of the great statesman, so much so that he would later commission a contrived group portrait of himself introducing his eldest surviving son, Jack, to the esteemed politician. He journeyed on to Dublin without his family and was consecrated at Christ Church Cathedral on the 31st of May 1767. Still short of money, he arrived at Cloyne to find his new diocese in poor shape and, for its lack of a south-facing room, the bishop`s house *'almost uninhabitable.'*

A sardonic joke of the period described the Church of Ireland as the church of the poor, because the poor paid for it. Everyone, of no matter what religion, had to give ten percent of their income towards the established church, a tithe that was bitterly resented by Catholics and Presbyterians, who could not afford decent buildings of worship for themselves, where these were even permitted. The Church of Ireland was riddled with placemen like Frederick, many of whom did little other than to pocket their salaries, if they bothered to live in their appointed parish. Therefore, little was expected of Frederick other than to take his money and uphold the status quo, but he was possessed of too much restless energy and intelligent self-interest to laze around. Now that he had finally gained a footfold, he intended to make something of it.

As an educated man from a political family, Frederick would already have had some grasp of Ireland`s affairs, but now he set about acquiring a deeper knowledge of the Irish people and their problems. Unusually for his time, he was religiously tolerant, since, as already noted, he had inherited his mother`s liberal mindset and was no great believer himself. From his grandfather, the 1st Earl, he also must have inherited some business sense, because over the next ten years – before he developed a real talent for spending it – he displayed great shrewdness in driving up his income.

Today, the landscape around Cloyne is a patchwork of green fields. The rock underneath is limestone, making it agriculturally rich. When Frederick arrived, the town was fringed by a large bog, which was treated as commonage by peasants for miles around, many not from Cloyne itself. Frederick discovered that the bog belonged to the church; improving this land would considerably boost his rents and rid the town of a persistent problem of disease. This was long before the science of microbiology, but people knew enough to understand that stagnant water was a source of ill-health.

Frederick hired men from the town and set about draining and fencing off the bog. However, cattle-herders who stood to lose pasture tore town Frederick`s fences, threw stones at his house, and assembled at his gates. Apparently the greatest resistance came from roguish types who were in the habit of driving stolen beasts onto the bog then claiming them for their own. Without overreacting, Frederick calmly faced down the protestors and the bog was successfully converted into decent farmland which even today, is still called Commons East and Commons West. Besides the land, Frederick set about improving the condition of his clergy, giving money to the more impoverished and initiating a policy of only appointing Irishmen to Irish posts. This was ironic, given his own provenance, but greatly endeared him to his new fellow countrymen. In another blessing, Frederick's wife, Elizabeth, gave birth to a daughter, Louisa, before the end of the year.

Early in 1768, the Bishop of Derry, Dr. Barnard, finally returned to the embrace of his maker. A popular but apocryphal story is told of Frederick playing leapfrog when he heard this news. Heaven only knows who a bishop might be playing leapfrog with, even one as feisty as Frederick, but the story goes that he stopped the game, exclaiming, *'I will jump no more. I have beaten you all, for I have jumped from Cloyne to Derry!'* A more believable version of this tale will be offered later, however with Barnard's passing, Frederick would indeed leap the entire length of Ireland.

A Derry bishop

It was a close call, because brother George had already resigned the viceroy's post and the new Lord Lieutenant, Lord Townshend, wanted to give the plum position to a candidate of his own choosing. However, in another instance of our hero's sheer good fortune, George III recalled that Frederick had been promised Derry and the king was a man of his word. So the appointment went to Frederick, a display of integrity that the monarch would live to regret.

The diocese of Derry was rich because it was big, comprising all of the county of Londonderry and parts of Donegal, Tyrone and Antrim. To set one matter straight at this juncture; the use of either 'Derry' or 'Londonderry' for both the city and county has long been a source of sectarian contention in Ireland. The official name of both city and county is still Londonderry, after the London guilds that developed the area in the 17th century. However, the Church of Ireland called the diocese 'Derry' at that time, and has since renamed it 'Derry and Raphoe.' For no other reason than convenience, Derry is used here (the name, incidentally, is an anglicisation of the Irish for 'oak grove').

When Frederick arrived in Derry in early 1768, he found a city of some 9,000 souls, less than one-tenth of today`s population. Precisely a hundred years previously, the city`s stone walls had resisted the armies of the Catholic King James II, but only now had a suburb begun spreading beyond those walls, the city`s port having made it an important stopover for the recent surge in transatlantic trade. Its inhabitants were mainly Protestant, vastly outnumbered by Catholics in its hinterland and Presbyterians on the nearby north coast. Not unlike Cloyne, at that time Derry must have seemed like the ends of the civilised earth, for beyond it lay only the vast Atlantic and the distant American colonies, then a voyage of some three weeks away.

Frederick was enthroned Bishop of Derry at Saint Columb`s Cathedral in March 1768. Conveniently, his palace was only a few paces away aross Bishop Street, within the walls. Saint Columb`s and the palace still stand to this day, although the latter was altered in Victorian times and its garden has been degraded to a car park. Just as he had at Cloyne, Frederick immediately set about winning hearts and minds. He visited all his parishes, ordering repairs to any dilapidated glebe houses that he found and initiating a pension scheme for any equally-dilapidated clergy. He continued his popular policy of only appointing Irishmen to Irish posts, but also, to the amazement of his Protestant flock, donated money to Presbyterian and even Catholic congregations for the improvement of their churches, which in the latter instance were often disused barns.

Although he privately called Catholicism *'a silly religion,'* his public display of tolerance was quite astonishing for its time. God was a touchy enough subject in England – which experienced anti-Catholic rioting in the 1780s – but in Ireland, divisions were (and still are) profoundly bitter. Again in private, Frederick was no more respectful of Presbyterianism; in one letter he wondered whether Presbyterians asked *'anything unreasonable when they desired to have their nonsense tolerated as well as any other nonsense?'*

As he became more powerful, his personal contradictions were amplified. The founder of Methodism, John Wesley, was Frederick's guest in Derry twice. Considering that Wesley was an evangelical revivalist and that his movement was being persecuted by Frederick's established church, one might imagine that he would have been quick to spot a bluffer. However, he said of Frederick: *'The Bishop is entirely easy and unaffected in his whole behaviour, exemplary in all parts of worship, plenteous in good works.'* Frederick could preach a good sermon, yet was capable of writing things like:

'If in this whirlwind I can direct the storm, so much the better for humanity but not for the lank-haired divinity nor the frizzle-topped divinity nor the hocus-pocus divinity.'

So he had little time for creeds, rather an eye for the bigger picture. Religion was something to be indulged, not fought over. Other more worldly preoccupations further endeared him to his new populace; he commissioned a spire for the cathedral; paid for mineshafts to search for coal in the area; but most importantly, promised to build Derry a bridge. The city's river, the Foyle, is wide and fast-flowing at that point and irregular ferry services were the only means of crossing. Frederick's bridge would not actually materialise for another two decades, but one commentator noted:

'Things of this sort rendered him the idol of his people and had a wonderful effect in conciliating the natives of that Kingdom, who are not apt to be over fond of the English Clergy.'

So pleased were the people of Derry with their new spiritual leader that they granted Frederick the freedom of the city. However, if Frederick was good for Derry, then Derry was good for him. An income of between £7,000 - £10,000 per year came with his new diocese, which again with astute management, he eventually succeeded in almost doubling. As already noted, the relative value of money is difficult to express over time, but by the retail price index, £10,000 then would be worth around £1.6 million today. It is perhaps more useful to think of it this way; in 1761, King George III bought Buckingham House – now Buckingham Palace – for £21,000. So from his Derry income alone, by the time he was 60, Frederick could almost have bought a residence like Buckingham House every year.

However, he was still only 38 and in almost no time at all, had been transformed from an anonymous, impecunious English clergyman into a popular and affluent Irish bishop. 1768 must have seemed a like very good year to Frederick, the only sad note being the death of his mother in September, at the age of 62. Still, given that she had enjoyed a happy widowhood and that, in a very practical way, he was exercising the liberal values that she had helped to nurture, Frederick accepted her loss philosophically.

A trip to Bath

1769 began less auspiciously, bringing with it two personal emergencies, both of which Frederick would seek to resolve by travelling to Bath. The Somerset spa town was then one of the most fashionable places in Britain, but Frederick had more pressing concerns than his public image. The first was gout, the illness which all the male Herveys seem to have inherited from their paternal grandmother, she of the Vesuvian mouth, who incidentally had died in 1741, *'of a fitt which seized her as she was taking the air in her Sedan in James's Parke'* (in London). Gout would lay Frederick low at regular intervals for the rest of his life; strictly speaking, it is a form of arthritis caused by too much uric acid in the blood, popularly characterised as a swelling of the feet that afflicts heavy drinkers. However, in the 18th century, the term was used to describe an entire dictionary of medical complaints that had yet to be categorised or even diagnosed; everything from genuine gout to stomach ulcers; bowel complaints; kidney, liver and heart disease through to cancer.

In an age where it was not unusual for a prosperous man to consume a plate of lamb chops and a bottle of wine for lunch every day, Frederick was actually quite healthy in his personal habits. He did not drink tea, believing (like his grandfather) that it was bad for the nerves and stomach. He certainly consumed meat and alcohol, neither to particular excess, although one acquaintance did observe that in company, '*he would drink a bottle of Madeira and swear like a gentleman.*' He went to bed early, rose before dawn and loved nothing better than a two-hour horseback ride before breakfast. He was a small, sprightly man, who carried little weight, but was nonetheless prone to abrupt bouts of illness. As his wife wrote: '*I think his constitution requires a slight fever now & then to purge it of the Vapours – it is like a chimney to Mount Vesuvius.*'

Still, his family often complained that his insistence on retiring by ten o`clock at night was an obstacle to their social lives, for during that era, most socialising happened in the home. When he built his first mansion, Frederick positioned his bedroom as far from everyone else`s as possible, at the end of its own wing.

However, he did drink port, so called because it was imported from Portugal and popular because it was relatively cheap, thanks to lower excise duty. It has since been discovered that for most of the 18th century, the Portuguese sweetened many fortified wines with lead acetate, which caused lead poisoning, some of the symptoms of which are abdominal pains and mental malaise. As he grew older, Frederick suffered from both.

Whatever the cause of his then current ailment, the cure was deemed a trip to Bath. The rudimentary medical knowledge of the period held that powerful healing could be derived from both drinking and immersing oneself in the hot, sulphurous spring waters that gave Bath its name. The spa`s beautiful architecture dates from this period, for by day, the ailing rich sought cures, but by night they sought luxury, entertainment, society and even marriage.

Frederick knew very well that amorous relationships often began in Bath and herein lay his second compelling reason for a trip. He had learned that his older brother, Augustus, had taken up residence there and had proposed marriage to a wealthy physician`s daughter, a Miss Moysey. Frederick did not want the union to proceed, because any male child it produced would impose a significant barrier between him and the glittering prize of the Hervey family fortune. Heaven forbid that anything should happen to Frederick`s esteemed eldest brother George, the 2nd Earl, but since he had remained childless, what had once seemed highly improbable now seemed more plausible, because Augustus, as yet, had no legitimate sons. The rich always like to get richer and by now, Frederick had become used to making his own luck.

Brother Augustus was about as different from the effete, delicate George as could be imagined and had little in common with Frederick either. He had, as already recounted, joined the Royal Navy as a boy. Like his father, he kept a diary that would not be published until long after he died. Whereas Lord Hervey`s journal gave an amusing insight into the court of George II, Augustus`s catalogued his maritime victories and his even more frequent onshore conquests. Known as 'the English Casanova,' Augustus had a talent for persuading women into bed, and all the better if they were married. By 1769, the crusty sea dog had retired from fighting and was following the family tradition of representing Bury in parliament, whilst at the same time seeking a post at the Admiralty. However, he had not retired from philandering; four years previously, he had sired an illegitimate son with a Lord of the Admiralty`s daughter, called Kitty Hunter. The boy was given his father`s name.

More scandalously, back in 1744, whilst still in his twenties, he had secretly married one Elizabeth Chudleigh, a maid of honour with a reputation for great beauty and not terribly much honour, who had once attended a ball wearing nothing but piece of transparent gauze. She sounds exactly the type the young Augustus would have gone for. Their relationship had lasted mere months and the two had lived apart ever since, but were still legally married. Elizabeth Chudleigh was Frederick`s secret weapon on his trip to Bath. As well as taking the waters, he wanted to keep an eye on Augustus and so be ready with damning evidence of the existing Mrs. Hervey, should his brother try to marry Miss Moysey. One can also be sure that after Frederick`s arrival, Miss Moysey`s respectable physician father got to hear of the suitor`s chequered past.

Augustus had hated Frederick for many years and now had even more reason. When both were young, he had found a note made by Frederick in a book *'which fixed me with regard to him.'* Augustus did not specify what Frederick`s note said, but the book was a French satire, lampooning different personality types. Had Frederick perhaps highlighted one that reminded him of his brother? Augustus`s family nickname was Coutchy, although it is not clear why (the word has a modern connotation that is best not mentioned). In 1754, when Frederick was still a budding clergyman, he had helped Augustus in his first parliamentary campaign. On that occasion, Augustus had lost and with typical wit, Frederick had declared that his brother had *'no more chance for his life at Bury than if he was already bury`d.'* The brothers were both Whigs, but agreed on nothing politically and had little in common personally.

However, at Bath, like any good sailor, Augustus could tell when the tide was turning against him, so he dropped his pursuit of Miss Moysey and never attempted to remarry again. He spent the rest of his days living mostly in Surrey and in London, with a former artists` model and courtesan called Mary Nesbitt, to whom he seems to have been faithful, perhaps having found his harbour at last.

Cured of his gout and victorious over Augustus, there was a bonus for Frederick when Elizabeth produced another boy, Frederick William. The trip to Bath had certainly been a beneficial one. Having spent only a year in his diocese, at this juncture Derry's new bishop might have been expected to return to his flock, but energised by his success, instead he pointed himself in the opposite direction; towards the continent, where he would spend the next two years. Vesuvius had almost brought his first trip abroad to an untimely end; on this occasion, he would nearly not make it home again.

A voyage of discovery

To her no doubt immense relief, Elizabeth Hervey was excused from this excursion. Instead, Frederick decided that his adventure of 1770 would be a masculine one, bringing only their eldest son Jack, who was then 12 and travelling abroad for the first time. In theory, Jack's young mind would be enriched by the experience of the Grand Tour and further improved by the company of Michael Shanahan, a Cork architect whom Frederick invited along to act as the boy's tutor. Frederick had met Shanahan during his stint at Cloyne; the Corkonian ran a business from his native city supplying architectural stone and would work for Frederick on Derry's cathedral spire, as well as on other, bigger projects, in an association that would prove both fruitful and highly fractious.

Besides educating Jack, Frederick had an additional motive for inviting Shanahan. This was long before the invention of photography and it will be remembered that Frederick was resolved to build a bridge for Derry. Shanahan would make detailed architectural drawings of bridges in other European cities, to identify an appropriate design. Also, Frederick wanted Shanahan to record volcanic rock formations, although in the event he hired other artists to do this as the architect's landscape sketches were not deemed up to scratch. Shanahan's drawings of bridges do survive though, in the form of engravings that include a dramatic flying arch proposal for Derry that unfortunately, was never built.

European travel in the 18th century was very different from the cosseted experience we enjoy today. For a start, the continent is now much more populous and developed, whereas two hundred years ago, entire tracts were still given over to wilderness, with agriculture often confined to the areas around fortified cities, towns and villages. Most people lived all their lives in their place of birth; the idea of travelling for pleasure was a contradiction in terms. A guide for Grand Tourists published nearly half a century after this particular trip advised readers to pack the following essential items; all their own bedding, including blankets and pillows, because inns either did not provide these or what they did provide, were disgusting; a well-stocked medicine chest, because finding a doctor could be difficult or impossible; oil of lavender, mosquito nets and a padlock, the oil and nets to deter insect parasites, the padlock to deter human ones because few inns had secure bedroom doors; a pocket-knife to eat with and a pair of pistols to see off highwaymen and wolves. At least one good carriage was also needed. Horses could be changed along the way, but even the small party of Frederick, Jack and Shanahan would have required a carriage; a cart for baggage; more than half a dozen animals and a similar number of servants including a cook, who travelled ahead to prepare meals. It was more akin to mounting an expedition.

Add to this the difficulties in obtaining travel permits, since English passports would not be recognised abroad until the following century. With the profusion of tiny statelets, particularly in what we now call Italy and Germany, new permits often had to be obtained for a journey of less than a hundred miles, as well as health certificates, if one had travelled from a city that had recently suffered an outbreak of infectious disease (like cholera, smallpox, tuberculosis or typhoid fever).

Then there was the problem of currency, which again varied hugely from state to state. It was dangerous to carry bags of coins, since this would attract thieves, so travellers like Frederick relied on letters of credit, sent from one's bank in England to various other banks en route. Postal systems could be erratic, so it was not unheard of to arrive in a new country and find oneself short of funds. However, there was a way around this for members of Frederick's class; letters of introduction, which one obtained before travelling and also picked up along the way. Thus, never having met or even heard of him before, a French, German or Italian nobleman could conceivably find Frederick on his doorstep, carrying a letter of introduction from some distant, mutual acquaintance. Etiquette required that the visitor be suitably accommodated and entertained. If such an encounter went well, the guest would be provided with a further letter of introduction for his onward journey and so on.

It has already been noted that European nobility shared not only the same privileged lifestyle but also the same educational background and values. Playing the generous host was one such value, even to the point where, if one happened to be away from home when a social equal called, servants were still instructed to provide a welcome and board. On his many journeys, aided by a lively personality and his fluency in Italian and French, Frederick perfected the art of introducing himself, whether he carried letters or not. Indeed, it became his habit when he arrived at any new destination to immediately call upon on the most important person in the vicinity. That way, he gradually melded with the cream of European society, but he also sought out artists, architects, scientists, writers and philosophers. He liked interesting people and many found him interesting and amusing in return. A well-travelled visitor also carried news and gossip, usually more recent than anything offered by the local journals (the predecessors of modern newspapers).

On this particular trip Frederick was not yet as famous (or notorious) as he would eventually become, so he used his new divine status to open many doors. Preoccupied with the question of religious tolerance, he visited Catholic monasteries and theological colleges to sound out his ideas. Such encounters were fruitful; Frederick became known abroad as 'le bienfaiteur des Catholiques' (bienfaiteur = benefactor). He even managed, when in Rome, to procure a private audience with Pope Clement XIV, no mean feat for a bishop who in the eyes of the Vatican, was a heretic. Relatively speaking, Clement was a liberal who desired peace in Europe and an understanding with England, which again, was a heretic nation. Frederick explained that he could ease the lot of Ireland`s downtrodden Catholics if, in return, they would swear loyalty to the English crown. A strict interpretation of doctrine dictated that Catholics should not recognise a non-Catholic monarch, since to do so was a denial of papal authority, but Clement was nonetheless receptive to Frederick`s suggestion. In turn, Frederick relished this sort of high politicking. He had no official sanction from his own church or state and certainly at this time, no other Protestant bishop behaved in such a manner, but through his efforts, he believed that he could lay the ground for genuine change. He also dropped in on his old friend Voltaire again; it is proof of his free-thinking spirit that he was on easy terms with both the head of the Catholic church and the high priest of religious scepticism.

When he was not visiting the great and good, Frederick indulged his new passion for vulcanology. The party travelled through France, Italy, Dalmatia (now Croatia), Austria and Switzerland, with first of all Shanahan sketching volcanic formations, then a series of local artists. In this prosaic manner, Frederick first found his feet as a patron of the arts. If one ever wonders what inspired his great love of travel, in spite of its difficulties, one should perhaps picture his little caravan crossing a beautiful, untamed landscape, at a time when Europe had no tarmac roads, no railways, no telegraph poles, pylons or suburban sprawl – none of the detritus of modern civilisation. It must have been a truly wonderful experience to wander the pre-industrial continent, with every new hilltop revealing another unspoiled vista. Sublime nature held a special place in the cultivated 18th century mind and the more awe-inspiring a prospect, the better. To cross an alpine pass, a carriage had to be taken apart, carried over in pieces and reassembled on the other side, but Frederick was oblivious to discomfort and usually rode horseback when he could. The rock formations that he wanted to study were often in isolated places and news of another monastery, ancient ruin, library or art collection was enough to send the expedition zig-zagging off in a different direction.

The travellers wandered in this carefree manner until the autumn of 1771, when Frederick suddenly fell ill in a remote corner of the Italian Alps. He lay close to the grave for almost a month, with symptoms resembling those of malaria (the disease was not eradicated from southern Europe until relatively recently). He was nursed by young Jack; Shanahan seems to have been off elsewhere, probably sketching bridges. Poor Jack was reduced to writing anxious letters to Peter, the 3rd Count de Salis, who had Irish blood and was one of the nobles to whom Frederick had recently introduced himself in the Grisons, then an independent canton but now part of eastern Switzerland. In his letters, Jack begged the count to send *'a dozen good lemons and… a very good Physician or doctor.'* The doctor (and presumably the lemons) duly arrived and by late October, although still very weak, Frederick had sufficiently recovered to descend from the mountains to the city of Verona, then part of the Venetian Republic, where he spent the winter.

Two pieces of news reached the party at Verona; firstly, that George III was less than impressed by the amount of time that the new Bishop of Derry was spending away from his diocese (this state of affairs would reverse itself in later years, when the king would welcome every moment that Frederick spent away from Ireland). Secondly, Frederick learned that Elizabeth had fallen ill, so he started for home, although not exactly at lightning speed. In a sign that his personal obsessions were now more important to him than either wife or king, he continued his geological researches and spent two whole months as a guest of the Catholic Archbishop of Rouen in France, furthering his plan for emancipation in Ireland. Finally, he sailed for Cork, and the Hervey family was reunited in Derry, in the autumn of 1772.

Domestic bliss in Derry

The Hervey girls found Derry boring, but then young Georgian ladies found anywhere that wasn`t London boring, since the capital was the epicentre of fashionable society. The tiny, faraway Irish city, with its deeply conservative inhabitants and frequent rain, must have seemed a dreary exile to Mary and Bess. Louisa was only 5 years old and no doubt content to be wherever her mother was. Still, the Bishop`s Palace within the city`s walls was commodious and had a nice garden. The church also owned an attractive deer park outside the walls, where Lumen Christi College is now located. Frederick had a summer house, or casino, built in the park, and when the weather was fine, the family would take a short carriage ride there for picnics. Georgian aristocracy promoted an idealised notion of rural living, encapsulated by the parklands created around stately homes, some of which survive today. Formal gardens did not completely disappear, but the custom was for wide, natural-looking vistas with strategically-positioned clumps of trees and water features or follies to catch the eye. Frederick`s casino (which means 'little house,' the term originally had nothing to do with gambling) was his first, tentative attempt to create a piece of heaven on earth.

Certainly, when the sun was shining, it must have seemed quite heavenly to linger amongst the birds, deer and trees. A family like the Herveys would never have had to work, either to earn money or even in the domestic sense. Servants took care of mundane tasks like doing the laundry, cleaning and preparing food. So it was a matter of filling the day with agreeable and preferably edifying pursuits. In the mornings, the children would have received their various tutors, studying a range of subjects like languages, the classics, literature and art, with a bit of mathematics or science for the boys and music for the girls. Afternoons were devoted to exercise through walking or riding, or when the weather was poor, to reading, and to writing letters.

Letters played a very important part in Georgian social life. It was quite usual to write a dozen in a day and when letters were received, they were often read aloud for family entertainment. Unless furtively exhanged, it was fully understood that letters were for popular consumption and so were written in a florid style, full of fine feelings, learned references and amusing asides that would hopefully reflect well on the sender. Noble families kept up their connections through letter-writing; it was crucial to know who was marrying whom, who was inheriting what, who was in favour at court and who not. It was also not uncommon for mail to be opened by government spies both at home and abroad and prudent letter-writers self-censored accordingly, or wrote in euphemisms on certain delicate subjects. For example, Frederick`s father had always been careful when writing to his male lover, Stephen Fox, for this very reason. On the other hand, effusive protestations of affection even between male correspondents were considered normal.

Besides letter-writing and reading, other amusements included games of cards, although that generation of Herveys seems to have avoided the scourge of heavy gambling that afflicted so many predecessors and peers. The children played music and sketched according to their talents and the family even had a resident artist of sorts in the shape of one Bitio, an Italian from the Dolomites, whom Frederick had employed to copy rock formations whilst abroad and brought back to Ireland to continue the task. Elizabeth described him as *'an honest though odd creature,'* perhaps in reaction to a portrait he painted of her and Louisa around this time (see photographs).

Labours of love

Frederick and Bitio spent the summer of 1773 exploring the north coast of what is now Northern Ireland. A popular tourist destination today, in Frederick's time it was remote and unfrequented. The angular, basalt formation called the Giant's Causeway was certainly known of, but attracted few visitors. Less well-known was the volcanic nature of the surrounding area, which Frederick was credited with bringing to wider attention, by distributing engravings of Bitio's sketches to his scientific contacts in Britain and Europe. Nearly a decade later, Frederick would be made a fellow of the Royal Society in recognition of his discoveries.

However, during his coastal explorations he discovered something else that would preserve his memory far beyond his now-forgotten scientific work. One day, riding on horseback, he came across a breathtaking headland. Behind lay heather-coated hills; beyond, the wide Atlantic, framed by north Donegal, the Causeway coast and on a clear day, the Scottish isles of Islay and Jura. The spot was called Downhill, from the Irish 'dun', meaning fort; an Iron Age mound nestled behind the headland. Something about Downhill struck Frederick, for soon, he would begin to spend a fortune on the place and eventually would make it his home. Yet many observers thought he was mad to plan a mansion *'where a tree is but a rarity,'* or as another put it, where *'only a romantic would expect to find a house, and only a lunatic would build one.'* Traditionally, stately homes were sited in lush locations, where the requirement of a picturesque view was balanced with the need to shelter from the elements. Downhill is all view and no shelter.

Perhaps one clue for Frederick's choice can be derived from the 18th century taste for the sublime; vast, romantic landscapes that dwarf the constructs of man. However, he had other considerations. From his base in Derry, the volcanic north coast that so fascinated him was a solid day's ride away and when one arrived, apart from a few tiny villages like Articlave and Bushmills, the only outpost of civilisation was the town of Coleraine, which was then so small as to make Derry seem like a seething metropolis and did not offer much in the way of luxury accommodation. Also, Downhill was church land and although his decision to build there may have seemed eccentric, it must be remembered that Frederick was no fool when it came to nurturing his assets. As yet, he had no land to call his own; the family estates were still beyond his reach and land was the basis of enduring wealth. So he hit on perfectly legal, if slightly complex and not exactly ethical-sounding way to accumulate some. When the lease on a portion of church land lapsed, it was usually renewed for a handsome payment to the incumbent bishop – in this case, Frederick. But if he chose not to renew the lease, he could forgo the payment and have the land held in trust, still collecting the rents but making it his for a set period, administered by trustees. As the scion of a landowning family, he would have known all the ploys.

Its land duly appropriated, Downhill was envisaged as that most modern of luxuries, a coastal holiday home. The first section constructed was an elegant villa, still easily discerned amidst the sprawling ruin left today (see photographs). The money to commence building came from brother George, who died suddenly at Bath in March 1775. Horace Walpole, the literary and political gossip who may have been related to Frederick as the illegitimate son of one of his uncles, wrote that George *'was born to the gout from his mother`s family, but starved himself to keep it off. This brought on paralytic strokes which have dispatched him.'* George left Frederick £10,000 and the family property passed to brother Augustus, who became the 3rd Earl of Bristol.

Another project close to Frederick`s heart came to partial, but much less satisfying fruition. In June 1774, in no small measure through his urging, royal assent was given to the Test Act, which allowed Catholics to swear allegiance to the king without betraying their spiritual allegiance to the Pope. Although the Penal Laws were still in place, barring Catholics from voting or owning property, this was seen as a first step towards official tolerance. The arrangement corresponded with the understanding that Frederick had built with many senior Catholic figures during his last continental journey, including Pope Clement himself. However, in a piece of rotten timing, the cultured Clement XIV died just three months after the Test Act was passed, to be succeeded by Pius VI, whose supporters were keen advocates of papal authority. The Catholic Bishop of Cashel near Cork had persuaded his clergy and congregation to take the oath, but after Vatican deliberation, all Catholics were forbidden from doing so and only a very small number took it regardless. Confronted with intransigence, Frederick remarked that: *'Rather than permit an abridgment of her privileges Rome would forgo a Toleration of her religion.'*

More domestic but equally-compelling matters also demanded his attention. By 1775, his eldest daughter, Mary, was 22 years old and his second, Bess, was almost 18. It was time for Mary in particular to be thinking of marriage, but in north-west Ireland, suitable husbands were in short supply. While a young aristocratic male was expected to make his own fortune, there was no question of a female ever assuming any occupation beyond that of loyal wife. Sometimes through inheritance, a woman could become independently wealthy, but the moment she married, her property became her husband`s. Frederick was now keen to get his daughters off his hands; after settling a dowry, they would then become someone else`s financial burden. Frederick was a much better parent than his father had ever been, but soon we will see a contrast emerge between his extravagant personal spending and his parsimony in relation to his own family.

Mary had already rejected a Cork gentleman and widower called Dominic Trant, who had been a guest of Frederick`s during a trip to inspect the Giant`s Causeway. Towards the end of 1775, she attracted another older suitor, the 45-year-old John Creighton, then Lord Erne, of Crom Castle in County Fermanagh (which still stands to this day). As Frederick wrote:

'He is a most unexceptionable man, who will have about £9000 a year, possesses a very beautiful seat in our neighbourhood, and is in love with her to the eyes. Unfortunately he is a widower and has children – this staggers her, and though I expect the conclusion before Christmas, yet perhaps after all it may go off.'

The children who staggered Mary and nearly put her off were two young sons and a 14-year-old daughter; at the age of 22, one can imagine how she felt at the prospect of becoming their stepmother. Still, a conclusion did materialise before Christmas and the couple were engaged, then married in February 1776. To her father's evident satisfaction, Mary became Lady Erne.

By this time, Bess was being wooed by one John Thomas Foster, a rector's son from Dunleer in County Louth. Although young, Foster was already a member of the Irish parliament and Frederick knew his father. Bess was prettier and livelier than her older sister; she was later described as *'a delightful creature, but ever so slightly naughty.'* Unlike Mary and Lord Erne, Bess and Foster seem to have been a genuine love match, although Frederick certainly approved of the relationship and the pair were married that April. In the space of just a few months, both Mary and Bess were established with husbands and Frederick was so pleased that he began doing what he always did when his spirits were up – planning another trip abroad. Every project he undertook seemed to hold such promise for the future and with boundless energy, he took Bitio off to the Western Isles of Scotland, to compare rock formations there with the Giant's Causeway.

The Grand Tour

It will be remembered that Frederick`s first trip abroad a decade previously had been a money-saving exercise, blighted by the death of his son George. His second had been a sort of Boy`s Own adventure. Now that he was a person of substance, his third would be a full-blown Grand Tour. His family would sally forth in style, to enjoy all that was edifying and to be seen in all the right places. Frederick, Elizabeth, Louisa (now 10 years old), Louisa`s governess, Bitio and several servants formed a sizeable core party whilst the newly-married Lord and Lady Erne travelled as far as Paris. Jack had followed his uncle Augustus into the Royal Navy and so was occupied elsewhere, as was Bess with Foster, and little Frederick William, still only 7 years old, was left behind in what turned out to be a wise move.

Perhaps Elizabeth had forgotten how much she disliked travelling, or perhaps she just wanted a break from Derry, but by the time the party reached Brussels, she was complaining of being *'mauled and suffocated by the heat.'* Then her hair began to *'fall out in handfulls.'* At Pyrmont – now Bad Pyrmont in central Germany – the weather changed to *'worse than you ever saw it, even in Derry, constant rain, dirt and puddle.'* With its mineral waters and unique 'vapours cave,' Pyrmont was then as fashionable as Bath, attracting nobility and other exotic visitors from all over Europe. Frederick enthused:

'Among this crowd are expatriated Prime Ministers, exhausted ministers of the gospel, Lutherans, Calvinists, Hernhuters (Bohemian Protestants), *Jews, Greeks &c., who altogether form a good savoury oglia of society, especially as one can pick out of the dish such pieces as are too luscious or too hard for one`s stomach, or even such as do not suit one`s palate.'*

He clearly thrived on these new encounters and dined regularly with Princess Augusta Frederica, King George III`s sister, *'quite en famille.'* The party then moved on to Stuttgart, now joined by the

Prince of Saxe-Gotha, whom Frederick described as: '*the first cousin of his Majesty George the third, King of Little Britain. He has better talents, more knowledge, and less pretension than most people – in short he is a most excellent companion and has all the appearance of a most affectionate friend.*' A real people person, Frederick was truly enjoying himself. Unfortunately, the same could not be said of Elizabeth. At Stuttgart she ominously wrote: '*I could never bear travelling, but nobody credits it.*'

To reach Verona in northern Italy – where Frederick had recuperated five years previously – the party had to cross the Alpine passes and the coach, Elizabeth`s scant source of comfort whilst in transit, was dismantled. Her husband adored the sublime mountains, but her misery only deepened:

'*Your Father you may imagine was in his element, my timid nature less at my ease; the weakness of my frame does not support objects of terror, my long journey, the heat, the buggs &c. sometimes bad Beds had robb`d me of some advantages which I had on leaving Pyrmont. Our present apartment is over ye stables, & Louisa is confin`d all day in ye stink.*'

By November 1777, the Herveys had reached Rome, where they settled for the winter in a more agreeable apartment than the one '*in ye stink.*' Elizabeth cheered up a bit, but not enough to socialise much and only received visitors twice a week. Her main past-times were to '*sit quietly by myself as usual, write to my dear Children and read my books.*' Seldom inclined to mope indoors, Frederick`s descriptions of the delights of Rome in his letters to Lady Erne show why, for the rest of his life, the lure of the Eternal City would prove so strong:

'*The conversations here are highly amusing, such is the equal mixture of cards and company. At one house we have a weekly concert accompanied with some tolerable voices; billiards are a favourite amusement in the evening. The English are upon the best footing imaginable, and of course well received everywhere, in apartments splendid beyond description and whatever magnificence can be deriv'd from Pictures, Gilding, Glasses, lights and multiplicity of Servants is all here exhibited. The morning especially is pass'd most deliciously – here is an incredible variety of admirable artists of every kind, so that one enjoys not only sculpture, painting & musick in the highest degree, but also sculptors, painters and musicians. 'Tis likewise difficult to say which pleases one most, the magnificence of ancient or the elegance of modern Rome.'*

He was hugely pleased when Pope Pius granted him permission to commission a copy of the famous statue of Apollo that stood in the Vatican's Belvedere courtyard – *'a favour rarely granted but to crown-heads.'* This copy would eventually grace his library at Downhill (although somewhere in transit, as Shanahan reported, it lost its *'nudities'*). Pope Pius, it might be remembered, had scuppered the Test Act in 1774, so it is worth noting that although the struggle for religious tolerance had by no means died in Frederick's breast, a passion for art was now growing that would eventually surpass it. He even tried to buy the Temple of Vesta at Tivoli, a Roman ruin which to this day, perches dramatically above a gorge. Ireland almost experienced its own version of the Elgin Marbles, since Frederick wanted to import the entire temple back to Downhill, but the papal authorities refused him permission (Frederick knew Lord Elgin, incidentally, and was unimpressed by him). He took the setback in his stride:

'Tis incredible how pleasantly I pass my time here. Your mother begins now to mix a little more, and I hope will gain both health and spirits by it; but she dares not attack palaces or antiquities, both on account of the fatigue and the damp. I am impenetrable to both, and besides have painters working in my room all the day. 'Tis really a life of Paradise. The set of English are pleasant enough and have their balls, their assemblies, and their conversaziones and instead of riots, gallantries (infidelities) *and drunkenness, are wrapt up in antiquities, busts & pictures.'*

With painters working in his room all day, Frederick's emerging vision of himself was that of *'a midwife to the talents.'* However, far from his idyllic Roman holiday, storm clouds were gathering that would greatly influence the next few years of his life.

The revolting colonies

Frederick had already noticed that touring French nobles were leaving Rome, a sign that something was afoot. Sure enough, in February 1778, France formally recognised the new United States of America and a month later, England declared war on France. The American War of Indpendence had begun three years previously, fuelled by England's attempts to tax its North American colony without sufficient political representation in return. In the time-honoured tradition of any foe of England being a friend, France had secretly been supplying the American Patriots and by 1778, the conflict was not entirely going England's way. Even at home, the war did not enjoy universal support; more enlightened commentators like Frederick saw England's governance as heavy-handed and discerned a degree of justice in the Patriot's cause.

In one letter he attributed *'the rebellious spirit in the central provinces of America to the exportation of nearly 33,000 fanatical and hungry republicans from Ireland in the course of a few years.'* Irish emigration to America, often portrayed as a Victorian phenomenon, had in fact been steady since the early 1700s. In Ireland, news of every battle was avidly followed, because resentments there precisely matched those of the American colonists. Also, the Irish parliament had sent 4,000 troops to America at England's request, leaving Ireland somewhat exposed.

An age-old English fear was of Ireland being used as a springboard for an invasion of the British mainland. Furthermore, should a foreign force land on Irish soil, oppressed Catholics would surely revolt. Some elements of the defeated Spanish Armada had attempted this tactic in 1588, then in 1601, Spain had landed 4,000 troops at Kinsale in Cork, with the ultimate aim of restoring Protestant England to Catholicism. As recently as 1759, during the Seven Years` War, the French had planned to invade the south coast of England. They didn`t, but the French privateer, Francois Thurot, had entered Belfast Lough with five ships and had taken Carrickfergus castle. England`s view of Ireland as a defensively weak back door was not unjustified; by 1778, American ships were even harassing the Royal Navy in Irish waters.

Events in America presented Ireland`s landowning Protestant Ascendancy with a dilemma. On the one hand, hostility from France posed a serious threat. On the other, Britain`s problems created an opportunity to wrest concessions; it might be remembered that the Irish parliament, which was the Ascendancy`s plaything, could pass no laws of its own and that Britain kept a tight control on Irish trade.

To keep the Ascendancy onside, Britain granted the Irish parliament more power and relaxed its grip on trade. To compensate for the shortage of British troops in Ireland, the Ascendancy founded the Volunteer movement. The Volunteers were a militia, not a professional army, but fuelled by a heady cocktail of patriotism and fear, ranks quickly inflated to almost 100,000, or twenty-five times the number of British soldiers who had left Ireland to fight in America. Ireland was swept by martial fever; the landowners had effectively raised their own private force. The Volunteers were overwhelmingly Protestant and swore allegiance to the British crown. Their job was to protect Ireland from a French invasion, which on this occasion did not come, so they held conventions and parades, drilled in public and issued proclamations. Far from being reassured, Britain`s representatives in Dublin Castle watched with mounting alarm. With no French invaders to fight, it did not require much imagination to see how this vast body of armed men might instead be used to wrest even more concessions. Liberal elements had admitted Presbyterians into the Volunteer ranks and even a very small number of Catholics, further stoking the debate over religious tolerance. The

Volunteers were led by James Caulfield, Lord Charlemont, of Marino House near Dublin. Charlemont was wealthy, cultivated and politically well-connected, but also incredibly pompous, so in many ways epitomised the Irish Ascendancy of that time. Soon, he would come to detest Frederick.

Our hero would have been aware of the deteriorating situation at home, but seemed in no hurry to leave his beloved Italy. However, he did befriend any French army officers lingering about Rome, treating them to ample dinners then playing the amateur spy, passing on military gossip on to his English political contacts, such as his old school chum, William Hamilton, the British ambassador in Naples. He also lectured anyone who would listen about the need for greater religious tolerance in Ireland, arguing with a strong degree of foresight that a more contented populace would be less amenable to either invasion or rebellion.

To escape the summer heat, the Herveys decamped to Castel Gandolfo, about fifteen miles outside Rome, but instead of finding relief, they all fell sick with malaria, which had nearly killed Frederick during his last trip abroad. This time, little Louisa very nearly died. She teetered on the brink until the autumn, before slowly recovering. Unwell herself and no doubt fraught with worry over Louisa, Elizabeth must nonetheless have been relieved that she had not brought along young Frederick William. Frederick himself suffered two bouts, but by November was avidly socialising once again and even more avidly collecting artworks for Downhill. Elizabeth nursed Louisa and in her letters to her older daughters, bemoaned the fact that, although he spent lavishly on art, her husband would not give her an allowance.

It would be the spring of 1779 before Frederick could tear himself away. Hostilities notwithstanding, the long journey home took the family through France, where Frederick met with that great founding father of the United States, Benjamin Franklin. Franklin was in Paris as an ambassador for his fledgling country and Frederick, true to his habit of seeking out the great and good, met with him four times. However, after about a month, something went wrong and the Herveys had to leave Paris quickly. Horace Walpole, who was not well-disposed towards Frederick and so has to be taken with a pinch of salt, wrote that he *'became so abusive of Dr. Franklin and the American Colonists that he was ordered to depart from Paris under pain of the Bastille.'*

A more likely version is that Frederick was at his amateur spying again. Whilst in Paris he wrote to Lord Germain, Britain`s hapless minister for America, about French plans to invade Ireland whilst pretending to aim for the Isle of Wight, off the southern English coast. So not only was this British aristocrat breezing around an enemy capital asking leading questions about military matters and talking freely with America`s most famous statesman, he also communicated his findings by letter, which he must have known could be intercepted. Whatever else, it showed enormous chutzpah, but no wonder the French told him to leave. He was lucky, on this occasion, that that was all they did. Still, by the end of 1779, after spending the autumn in England, the Herveys were safe home in Derry.

The Earl Bishop

Within weeks of Frederick`s return to Ireland, brother Augustus, the 3rd Earl of Bristol, died from gout of the stomach. Frederick became the 4th Earl of Bristol and England`s first Earl Bishop since 1067, when Odo, Bishop of Bayeaux and half-brother of William the Conqueror, was made Earl of Kent. As well as his title, Frederick inherited Ickworth, estates in Essex and Lincolnshire and the London townhouse in St James`s Square. Augustus only passed on the entailed property, which by law had to go to the next male heir. He hated Frederick so much that he even gave away the deer in Ickworth Park. Still, on paper Frederick`s wealth more than doubled. Along with his diocesan income, he was now worth between £30,000 and £40,000 per year, or between £4.8 and £6.4 million, although modern monetary values do not adequately communicate Georgian spending power – it always worth recalling the example of Buckingham House selling for £21,000 in 1761.

We might also recollect the rather improbable story of Frederick playing leapfrog in Cloyne and claiming to have won the game by leaping to Derry. The more likely version is; quite a few years after he became the 4th Earl, Frederick saw a young tenant farmer near Downhill, making extraordinary jumps to impress his friends. He is said to have saluted the peasant athlete thus:

'Well, you certainly have made a grand jump, but in my time I have made three jumps, and I think each of them better than yours. I was a curate, and I jumped into the bishopric of Derry; I was a commoner, and I jumped into the earldom of Bristol; I was a younger son and landless, and I jumped into the Bristol estates – not bad jumps, eh? I think I got further than you.'

He was right; the past decade had been dizzying, the 18th century equivalent of winning the lottery. Frederick had been a man of no wealth or position until his mid-thirties, but by his late forties, was worth a fortune and was moving at the highest levels of British and European society.

By now, his coastal villa at Downhill was taking shape, with a few rooms almost habitable, but his new status – and more pressingly, his new art collection – needed something more. Although he now owned Ickworth Park, he maintained that he did not want to build there, because the soil was too damp and the air did not agree with him. So began in earnest the development of what surely was the most unusual mansion and demesne in the British Isles. Even at the height of its glory, Downhill was not exactly beautiful – but it was exceptional.

For the next decade, Frederick and his architect Michael Shanahan would bicker almost non-stop as they collaborated on this quixotic project. Frederick was the client from hell; demanding endless extensions and changes, spending a fortune yet querying every penny, even at one time sending in an Italian architect over Shanahan`s head. Shanahan regularly stormed off the job and in turn argued constantly with the chief stonemason, James McBlain. Yet on the windswept headland, these very different men achieved something quite extraordinary.

Goodness knows what the locals made of Frederick at first, building a palace in a place barely fit for grazing sheep. As one visitor later wrote, *'never have I seen so bad a house occupy so much ground.'* However, Frederick brought decades of employment and improvement to a hopelessly marginalised area, for as well as his mansion, he commissioned roads, walls, bridges, even a waterfall and a lake. The entire upper headland was cleared of rocks and heather, then planted with trees and grass. At one point, Frederick boasted that he had 150 men working on the park alone and that at Downhill, *'a tree is no longer a rarity,'* because he planted many thousands. He introduced new farming methods and took an interest in his tenants; no wonder he was liked by the ordinary people. As ever with Frederick, his eye was on the bigger picture: *'If we employ the idle, they will make no riots, and if we can fill their bellies, they will no more open their mouths.'*

No less amazing than the house itself were the contents; Frederick crammed Downhill with antique statues and paintings by artists that nowadays, would rarely be found outside the most prestigious galleries. Back then, to have seen works by Rembrandt, Durer, Rubens, Titian and Tintoretto, hanging in the middle of nowhere, beside a wild Atlantic cliff, must have been mind-boggling. Around the demesne, he planned a series of eye-catching structures, modelled on some of his favourite classical buildings. The first was in homage to his late brother, George. Called the mausoleum, although it does not house George`s remains, it contained a statue to him. A version of a Roman monument in Saint Remy de Provence, it stood for only 60 years, before the upper half was blown down in a storm, in 1836. The falling stonework apparently killed a rabbit and George's head somehow disappeared, never to be found again. His statue – minus its head – is still at Downhill, lurking behind a hedge. The inscription around the mausoleum's plinth is from the Roman poet Virgil, and translates as: *He gave my oxen, as you see, to stray, and gave me my ease, my favourite tunes to play.*' It was true; George, who had never set foot in Ireland, let alone Downhill, had made all this possible, and Frederick was truly grateful. However, no statue was ever raised to Augustus.

In the meantime, there was the other major matter of taking on the English estates and settling Augustus's will and debts, but Frederick preferred to supervise his earthly paradise at Downhill and sent Elizabeth to Ickworth in his place. Not the least of her problems was to start paying back the £10,000 loan that Frederick had arranged upon inheriting. At this stage, much of his wealth was on paper only and he had spent huge sums of money collecting art in Italy and on his extraordinary Irish treasure-house. From her letters, it can be judged that Elizabeth did not share Frederick's passion for Downhill. And when her daughter Mary, Lady Erne, wrote to her at Ickworth complaining that she had nothing in common with her own husband, Elizabeth replied: '*As to Lord Erne – I believe he is like Lord B. (Frederick); too difficult to be long pleased.*'

Soon afterwards, Elizabeth's mother, Lady Davers, died at Bury. At least Elizabeth was close by, instead of stuck in some faraway corner of Ireland or Italy. One cannot help wondering whether at this stage, she recalled her mother's initial opposition to Frederick. Lady Davers had had a very strong personality; in her will she specified that she did not want to be buried with her husband, rather in a plain coffin, like a pauper, at the foot of her parents' grave.

Now the mistress of Ickworth Lodge, Elizabeth had a little house demolished at the edge of the park; the cottage that she and Frederick had lived in, during the early years of their marriage.

Unhappy families

Mary, who was now 27, had married a man just one year younger than her father. Her personality was similar to her mother`s – placid and dependable – and she had just given birth to a daughter, little Caroline. However, she had never truly been in love with Lord Erne and now found him fussy and boring. What she thought of her three stepchildren is not recorded. The couple had taken a house in Dublin, where Lord Erne had assumed a role with the Volunteers, and she was joined there by Bess, who was equally fed up with her own married life in Dunleer. Even with her sister for support – or perhaps, having to support her sister whilst at a low ebb herself – Mary could not settle and grizzled constantly in her letters to her mother. There was no name for it then, but she may have been suffering from post-natal depression. In the spring of 1780, her mother suggested getting out of Dublin, which was not regarded as a healthy place, and going to stay with Frederick in Downhill to benefit from the sea air. Mary did so, taking her baby girl with her.

Bess, who was still only 22, could not bear to return to her husband, John Foster, in Dunleer and so decided to follow Mary. The Herveys referred to Foster as *'Little f'* and it seems as if *'Little f'* had developed some unsavoury habits, which included treating Bess harshly, allegedly forcing himelf upon her and having an affair with her maid, a Madame Wagniere. The couple already had a two-year old son (called Frederick) and now Bess was pregnant again. However, when she too showed up at Downhill, she found her father less than sympathetic. Bess was more glamorous than Mary, but Mary was Frederick`s favourite. Or perhaps, preoccupied with his grand schemes, he did not want another distressed daughter about the place.

Callously, he told Bess to return to Foster. A modern-day writer of television soaps would be hard pushed to devise a better plot, but this was nothing compared to some of the situations Bess would later create for herself.

She was so repelled by Foster that she instead fled to her mother at Ickworth. On the way, she met up with a Mr Churchill, who escorted her to Scotland and then as far as York, before Foster caught up with them. Mr Churchill may have been more than just a gallant friend; either way, he was rapidly dispensed with and the warring couple continued on to Ickworth. Bess`s older brother, Jack, had arrived there before her, returned from naval service in Canada. Jack was now 23, and had acquired a wife in Quebec, a quiet girl called Elizabeth Drummond, although he himself had developed into a hot-headed type. As a child, he had been very close to Bess and passing through Dublin on his way home, he had heard all the stories about how Foster was treating his little sister. So by the time Bess and Foster reached Ickworth, Jack had primed their mother. She found Bess *'the picture of woe, & despair, her health ruin`d, & all her prospects blasted,'* and declared that Foster was the *'detestation of everybody.'* Whatever about Foster`s character, it must have been intimidating to face a house full of hostile Herveys.

Perhaps because he had been a friend of Foster`s father; perhaps because he was now so immersed in Downhill that he did not appreciate what was happening with his family; perhaps because he was being selfish and did not want Bess to become a financial drain on him again; perhaps because of her dalliance with Mr Churchill or indeed perhaps for all of these reasons, Frederick commanded that Foster be allowed to stay at Ickworth, to attempt a reconciliation. This did not go well. In his mother-in-law`s eyes, Foster was *'more absurd & inconsistent than it is possible to express… a ship totally without ballast, blown about by every gust of passion, a very tiring companion and unsatisfactory friend.'* Of Bess, she opined, *'I believe nothing can remove her disgust.'* Foster could only stomach so much of this and eventually sloped off to London. Shortly afterwards, his affair with Madame Wagniere became common knowledge, although interestingly, she too would claim that *'Little f'* had forced himself on her. Bess gave birth to another son at the start of December.

Then Mary turned up with Lord Erne. Unlike the Fosters, for the time being, the Ernes had patched up their differences. Finally, Frederick managed to rip himself away from Downhill and he arrived at Ickworth just before Christmas. The Lodge must have been packed; it was the first occasion in five years that Frederick`s immediate family found itself under the same roof. No-one knew it then, but it would also be the last.

The art of falling apart

The year 1781 started agreeably enough, with plenty of socialising, excursions and visits from relatives. Foster even returned to Ickworth for one more attempt at reconciliation, but by May it was clear that Bess`s marriage was irretrievably over and, if such a thing was possible, *'Little f'* had sunk even lower in Elizabeth`s eyes: *'he is in all things ye mud of ye streets.'* However, by spurning her husband, Bess was not choosing an easy path. In those days, divorce was very difficult and each individual case required an Act of Parliament. Even for the wealthy, a private separation was the only realistic option and the husband had an automatic right to keep any children, unless otherwise agreed. Foster kept the children. They would be raised in Ireland and, once she handed them over that summer, it would be nearly fifteen years before Bess saw her sons again.

By then, Mary`s marriage had also played itself out, although with less acrimony; Lord Erne allowed her to keep their daughter, Caroline. The two sisters went to Bath, where they could live cheaply compared to London and console one another. Women in their situation occupied a sort of social limbo; for the first few years of separation at least, they could not be courted by any gentleman who valued his reputation and had to survive off whatever allowance – if any – the estranged husband might give. Bess`s mother had extracted an agreement from Foster to pay Bess £600 per year, but in the event she saw little of it. On the same subject, Frederick`s reputation would now take a severe dent. According to one relative:

'Never was a story more proper for a novel than poor Lady Elizabeth Foster`s. She is parted from her husband, but would you conceive that any father with the income he has should talk of her living alone on a scanty pittance as £300 a year! And this is the man who is ever talking of his love of hospitality & his desire to have his children about him… It is incredible the cruelties that monster Foster made her undergo with him; her father knows it, owned him a villain, & yet, for fear she should fall on his hands again (ie. cost him money), *tried at first to persuade her to return to him.'*

The forsaken woman was a popular fictional heroine of the time and Bess certainly lived up to the role. With her children taken away and just £300 a year from Frederick to live on (which again, she had trouble extracting), her future was far from bright. However, just when she seemed consigned to what even the loyal Jack called *'A Gloomy Dismal Fate,'* fate itself intervened in the shape of two unexpected visitors. Fashionable society descended seasonally on Bath, in search of cures but also amusement. Bess`s story had spread like wildfire amongst the nobility and because she was young and pretty, she had gained a certain unfortunate cachet. One day, a maidservant opened the door of the rented house she shared with Mary, to admit William Cavendish, the 5th Duke of Devonshire, and his wife, Georgiana.

The Devonshires were the golden power couple of their age. Handsome and hugely wealthy, they occupied the pinnacle of London political and social life. The palatial Devonshire House in Piccadilly was a regular meeting place for Whig grandees and a venue for endless salons, soirees and balls. The Duke owned property all over Britain and Ireland; Devonshire House was demolished in 1924, but Chatsworth House in Derbyshire is still home to the present Duke and is one of England's finest mansions. The 5th Duke was a languid sort but his wife, Georgiana Spencer, sparkled with energy and was widely adored. She knew the Prince of Wales (the future George IV) well enough to decribe him as *'too fat and looks like a woman in men's cloaths.'* As to why they bothered calling with the hard-up Hervey girls, Georgiana later said that they did so to shame Frederick into helping them. She thought him *'a strange man.'*

However, there was another factor at play, for behind their glittering façade, the Devonshires were bored. When he wasn't enjoying his mistress, a humble clergyman's daughter called Charlotte Spencer (no relation to Georgiana), the Duke spent most of his time at his London club. He had already had an illegitimate daughter by Charlotte and Georgiana in her turn would have an illegitimate daughter, by the 2nd Earl Grey. Georgiana was a problem gambler, losing huge sums of money then attempting to hide her debts from the Duke; her habit would get worse. The Devonshires sucked Bess into their convoluted relationship; she would, in the future, bear two illegitimate children by the Duke, on both occasions going abroad to give birth, leaving the child with foster parents then returning to live with the couple, with Georgiana none the wiser. It is amusing that Georgiana should have thought Frederick *'a strange man,'* for it has been rightly said of the menage a trois that developed between Bess and the Devonshires that *'no trio could be stranger than theirs.'* They called one another by intimate nicknames; because he liked dogs, the Duke was Canis; because of her big eyes, Bess was Raccy, short for raccoon; and for reasons known only to themselves, Georgiana was Mrs. Rat.

Bess has sometimes been portrayed as a leech, insinuating herself into the Devonshire's marriage and destroying it from the inside. It was said of her that she had *'all the wit, all the subtlety, all the charm and all the wickedness of the Herveys.'* Many years later, after Georgiana died, she would marry the Duke, becoming the Duchess of Devonshire herself. However, she was not a calculating siren, nor did the Duke impose Bess on Georgiana as his 'other woman' (a further version of events, portrayed in a 2008 film starring Kiera Knightley). It was Georgiana who first took to Bess and the two would become intimate, lifelong friends. That first summer of 1781, Georgiana invited the penniless Bess to Plympton near Plymouth, where the Duke, who was an officer in the Derbyshire Militia, had to attend to military duties. Georgiana had married the Duke six years previously at the age of 17 and had suffered a number of miscarriages. One of the pressures in their relationship was her apparent inability to produce an heir. As an excuse to make Bess part of their household, the Devonshires employed her as a governess to the Duke`s daughter by Charlotte Spencer, also called Charlotte, who lived with the couple. A noblewoman working as a governess to an illegitimate child was deemed a disgrace and even more disapproval fell on Frederick`s head as a result. However, most of these events had yet to unfold and whilst Bess went off to Plympton, Mary and her daughter, Caroline, stayed on in Bath.

Meanwhile, Frederick spent most of 1781 and 1782 visiting social contacts and intellectual figures all around England, his desire for stimulating company undiminished (and possibly heightened) by the family dramas unfolding about him. Although he professed not to like living at Ickworth, he held regular dinners there, which were very masculine affairs. One regular guest, the writer Arthur Young, greatly enjoyed them:

'Lord Bristol was one of the most extraordinary men I ever met with. He was a perfect original – dressed in classical adorning; he had lived much abroad, spoke all modern languages fluently, and had an uncommon vein of pleasantry and wit, which he greatly exerted, and without reserve, when in the company of a few select friends. In my life I never passed more agreeable days than these weekly dinners at Ickworth.'

However, the agreeable dinners at Ickworth were about come to an end.

A bad father and a worse husband

One day in the middle of November 1782, Frederick and Elizabeth took a carriage ride around Ickworth Park, the sort of gentle outing that middle-aged couples regularly make. When they returned, they never spoke again; after thirty years of marriage, a rift had opened that would never heal. Within a week, Frederick stormed off to Ireland and Downhill, whilst Elizabeth stayed on at Ickworth with only Louisa for company, who by that time was 15.

Then as now, marital breakdown is usually about lots of things, brought to a head by one. Although the coachman could never be induced to say what had happened on that ride, from subsequent letters of Elizabeth`s, a disagreement over the St James`s Square townhouse in London seems to have been the catalyst. Elizabeth liked staying there and in her own quiet way had used it for entertaining the previous year, whilst Frederick had flitted around the country in his usual restless manner. She was keen to spend the season of 1783 in the house, because Louisa would then be 16 and have her social coming out. Allowing for breaks at Christmas and Easter, the London season opened in November, with the king`s speech in parliament and lasted until the summer, when the stench of the city drove the wealthy back to their country seats. The seasonal whirl of dinner parties and balls were perfect for introducing young ladies of Louisa`s age onto the marriage market.

However, Frederick had unilaterally decided to rent St James`s Square to one Lord Paget for £600 for a year. Although rich on paper, he was always short of ready cash. Trundling along in the carriage, one can imagine how the disagreement went from there, with Frederick lecturing Elizabeth about his favourite subject with regard to her – the need to economise. Although he spent vast amounts on art and architecture, he was not, as already noted, particularly generous when it came to his own family. Although she was arguing on Louisa`s behalf, not her own, when Elizabeth begged him for the use of the house, Frederick fell to abusing her for vanity. In return, she called Frederick selfish; the thorny subject of travel probably came up and possibly even the death of their first son, George. Frederick wanted their youngest son, Frederick William, to spend time with him in Ireland, but Elizabeth did not want to let him go.

Marital strife blasted the Herveys to pieces. The cliché that money does not buy happiness certainly was true in this instance. When Frederick had been a humble clergyman, his family had been poor but content, living in their little Horringer cottage. Now he was rich, but his grandsons through Bess had gone to the despised *'Little f'* in Ireland, whilst Bess herself was a dependent of the Devonshires. Mary was also without either money or a husband and moping at Bath. Jack had not only followed his uncle Augustus into the Royal Navy, but was acquiring a similar reputation for philandering, which his quiet and subservient wife was powerless to prevent. Louisa and young Frederick William could only watch as their father abandoned their mother at Ickworth, denying her the means to enjoy any sort of social existence. He even refused to let her keep horses, in an age when any lady of consequence needed a coach just to get around. The abruptness and finality of their separation was certainly a surprise, although many years later, a great-grandson would write:

'The wonder is not that they departed now, but that they had gone on together for so long. For the Bishop's virtues, such as they were, were of a public and not of a private kind. They consisted of enlightened views on public questions, rather than those virtues which conduce to the happiness of a home.'

It was the bumptious Lord Charlemont, the head of the Volunteer movement, who later labelled Frederick *'a bad father and a worse husband.'* In an ugly metaphor for what was happening to the Herveys, Augustus's illegitimate son, also called Augustus, was killed at sea that same month, blown apart by a cannonball.

Beautiful Frideswide

Whatever about poor Elizabeth, Frederick did not remain in low spirits for long. By March of 1783, he was sending chirpy letters from a house called Larchfield, set in the rolling countryside near the pretty village of Hillsborough, in County Down. Larchfield still stands to this day and was then home to a family called Mussenden, and in particular to a girl called Frideswide Mussenden. Frideswide was Frederick`s cousin once removed; her mother was Frederick`s cousin, Henrietta, a daughter of uncle Henry Hervey-Aston, the former rakehell who had been so kind to Samuel Johnson. Henrietta had married a Scotsman called James Bruce, but had died young, and over the years, Frederick had taken a passing interest in her children. Now, as he became alienated from his own children, his interest was rekindled.

From Frideswide`s portrait (see photographs), it can be seen that she was still barely more than a child. There is doubt over her precise year of birth; it is given by some sources as 1763 and by others as 1765. However, since the birth year of one of her two older brothers is also tentatively given as 1763, the second date is the more likely, which would have made her 18 at this point. Beyond doubt was her beauty, for which she was renowned. In that era, it was quite normal for girls to be married in their late teens and young as she was, Frideswide already had an infant son. Her unusual name, incidentally, derives from the patron saint of Oxford. The 53-year-old Frederick had another name for her; his *'chere cousine.'*

'I have not known for months together, what a gloomy cloudy moment meant. Eternal springs & cloudless skies have been the unremitting appanage of this chere cousine`s innocent spirits, gay society and indefatigable attentions to me, indeed nothing can pass more deliciously than our time ever since we have liv`d so much together, tho` we are never separate until eleven at night, yet the Slumbers pure. At breakfast the chere cousine presides, & the very effulgence of her dear innocent countenance is sufficient to animate

& enliven all around her. From breakfast we retire to the Harpsichord, where I have the singular privilege of being admitted comme un bon Papa.'

Un bon Papa, indeed. Frederick was smitten, or at the very least experiencing what we would nowadays call a mid-life crisis. He may have been rich, related, a bishop and a house guest, but his behaviour did not go unremarked by Frideswide`s husband, Daniel Mussenden, who was then in his thirties. Frederick returned to Downhill that April, to commission the famous temple on the cliff, which under much less happy circumstances would later be given the name of his *'chere cousine.'*

Frederick the warrior

Besides Frideswide, Frederick succumbed to another infatuation upon his return to Ireland. In 1783, the American War of Independence was drawing to a close and England had already agreed a peace with France. However, in Ireland, the Volunteer militia that had assembled to defend against a French invasion showed no sign of disbanding. On the contrary, the Volunteers were more popular than ever and, having transcended their original purpose, were being used by the landowning Protestant Ascendancy to win concessions from Britain. Much to Britain`s annoyance, it had been forced to relax its stranglehold on Irish trade and to abolish the law that made the Irish parliament subject to the English one.

Nonetheless, the Irish parliament was still hopelessly corrupt and easily influenced. The Lord Lieutenant, or English viceroy, also controlled the executive branch of government and could manipulate politicians through patronage, awarding titles to those who did his bidding. This meant that the concessions won by the Volunteers looked better on paper than they worked in practice. So the next goal of this well-armed, well-disciplined pressure group was no less than complete parliamentary reform, a prospect that Britain dreaded, since an Irish parliament with a mind of its own would be impossible to steer. Indeed, even the Protestant Ascendancy was beginning realise that, in the Volunteers, it had created something of a monster.

Frederick had previously been lukewarm about the militia, but during the summer of 1782, had sent a few admiring letters to the chairman of the Londonderry corps. Although he was a latecomer, the admiration proved mutual. Frederick donated some new equipment, then joined the Londonderry Volunteers and quickly rose to the rank of Colonel. After all, the Bishop of Derry and 4th Earl of Bristol was the most socially important person in the county and even though he was away a lot, having him as a figurehead was a coup.

For his part, Frederick had long believed that defeating religious discrimination was the key to solving Ireland`s problems. Some Volunteer battalions admitted Presbyterians and a few members even argued that the only way to fully reform parliament was to end Catholic oppression. This was music to Frederick`s ears. He developed a sudden appetite for military pomp, dressing up in uniforms, attending parades, receiving and making noble addresses. He had the Iron Age fort at Downhill blown up, the one that gave the estate its name, to create a flat surface for visiting milita to parade on. He ordered a new gate built for the demesne, called the Coleraine Battallion arch (which still stands, but is now called the Bishop`s Gate). He attended a convention held at Dungannon in September 1783, at which it was decided to hold a Grand General Convention in Dublin, for all the Volunteers in Ireland. A force of thousands of heavily-armed men descending on the capital to press for political reform was just about the last thing that the British establishment wanted.

At the time, it was suggested that Frederick had tried to persuade the same British establishment to appoint him Lord Lieutenant of Ireland and that his enthusiasm for the Volunteers was a reaction to being turned down. He definitely saw himself as someone who could unite this quarrelsome country; he was an English aristocrat, but loved by the Irish; he was a Protestant bishop, but respected by all faiths. Becoming viceroy would have been an extraordinary leap, but his brother had held the post and by now, Frederick was accustomed to making extraordinary leaps. Perhaps, with his eye for the bigger picture, he saw this as his defining moment; perhaps he saw himself in the mould of the Roman statesmen whose statues he collected; perhaps, recalling his visit to Corsica in 1766, he envisaged himself in the role of patriot and liberator, just like Pasquale Paoli. He certainly behaved that way. His progress to Dublin for the Grand Convention in November 1783 was nothing short of spectacular; accompanied by ranks of Volunteers and guarded by sentries, he was met with jubilant civic receptions in every town along the way. He must have felt like a true people`s hero. His entrance to the capital was described thus:

'The Bishop of Derry arrived in town this day, escorted by a squadron of Derry Volunteers. The Right Reverend Father in God wore a purple coat faced with white, and on his head a gold laced hat with a cockade. He was received at Lord Charlemont`s by different corps of Vounteers under arms, and takes up residence at Mr. Fitzgerald`s, who went out to meet him this morning in great pomp and splendour. "Long live the Bishop!" echoed from every window; never did there appear so extraordinary a procession within the realm of Ireland.'

The Mr. Fitzgerald mentioned was Frederick`s nephew; it may be remembered that he had a sister called Mary who had married a rascally squire in County Mayo, before fleeing back to England in the 1750s. Her son was now a 35-year-old man; handsome and dashing, George Robert Fitzgerald had been educated at Eton, joined the army at 17, and had been a favourite at the French court. However, he was even more rascally than his father and was commonly known by his sobriquet, 'the Fighting Fitzgerald,' owing to the numerous duels he had started and won, although he had once been shot in the skull, which some say, made his behaviour worse. At home in Mayo, he kept a bear as a pet and hunted by torchlight, runnning riot around the countryside with a band of henchmen. Now, he was heading up a corps of Volunteers, and had placed his townhouse in Merrion Square at his uncle's disposal. There, Frederick set about wining, dining and conniving with the other Volunteer commanders as they arrived in Dublin. His aims were no less than the complete reform of parliament, the toleration of Catholics and if necessary, personal control of the entire Volunteer movement. One way or another, he intended to make Ireland a better place, but conceivably, vanity may also have played a part.

Lord Charlemont, the leader of the Volunteers, disliked Frederick intensely. The two men had a lot in common, including a love of travel, art and architecture, but whereas Frederick was quick-tongued and showy, Charlemont was a nervous blusterer. Charlemont also knew exactly what Frederick was up to and did not intend to let this popular upstart push him aside. He furthermore did not think the Grand Convention a good idea, but his organisation was very keen on it, so he had to go through the motions. He vehemently opposed giving Catholics any relief whatsoever. In his memoirs, his hatred of Frederick is palpable:

'Possessed of no one firm principle, public or private, he is continuously assuming and as constantly forfeiting the character of a patriot and of a virtuous man… his genius is like a shallow stream – rapid, noisy, diverting, but useless… to the Papists, from his long residence in Popish countries, he was, I believe, sincerely addicted.'

Balanced against that description is another, from a more appreciative observer at the time:

'Rather under middle size, he was peculiarly well made, his countenance fair, handsome and intelligent, but rather expressive of a rapidity of thought than of the deliberation of judgement – his hair receding from his forehead gave a peculiar trait of respectability to his appearance. His manners appeared zealous and earnest… he could not

be viewed without an impression that he was a person of talent and eminence.'

Amidst much excitement and intrigue, the Grand Convention got under way at the Rotunda, which still stands near the top of Dublin's O'Connell Street (then called Sackville Street). 160 delegates packed the building and fresh from his glory in the streets, Frederick expected to be elected president, but Charlemont quickly trumped him there. Frederick then tried speechifying from the floor, arguing passionately and persuasively. Even Charlemont admitted that he was *'warmly supported by many of the Connaught and some of the Munster delegates, while even the Northern Dissenters, by their speeches and acquiescence, appeared already to indicate the approaches of that strange madness by which they were not long after actuated.'* By 'strange madness', Charlemont meant fighting for religious tolerance, which shows what an outlandish concept he considered it.

Frederick hoped that the convention would quickly agree a set of demands and submit these to the Irish parliament, sitting half a mile away across the River Liffey. With such a large number of armed men marching around town, parliament would need to take any such demands seriously. However, using agents of influence, the British administration sabotaged the conference from within. Charlemont and the great Protestant politician Henry Flood, who was also a Volunteer and an opponent of Catholic emancipation, managed to quash tolerance as a key demand.

What had started with such promise became bogged down in division and dragged on for nearly three weeks. To the satisfaction of the British and Irish parliaments, the Grand Convention was neutralised. Frustrated, Frederick returned to Derry, again meeting civic receptions on the way. He based himself at Downhill, where he received addresses from Volunteer corps who continued to see him as a great leader. Some of his replies were remarkably violent for a bishop and an earl who was, after all, ostensibly an establishment figure. One such, published in July 1784, read:

'Whenever a rapacious oligarchy shall impose laws subversive of the liberties, and levy taxes contrary to the will of the people; it then behoves that people to repel the tyranny and exterminate the tyrants.'

Frederick was effectively accusing King George III of tyranny and encouraging a violent revolt. The king was furious, particularly stung since he had, it might be remembered, installed Frederick as Bishop of Derry on a point of honour. Now, he called Frederick *'that wicked prelate.'* The Lord Lieutenant in Dublin drew up a warrant for Frederick's arrest, for seditious conduct, which potentially carried the death penalty, but could at least have led to a spell in prison. Spies were sent to Derry to watch Frederick's behaviour and it was suggested that he might even arm a Catholic militia. Frederick had never been more popular, but he was finding that fame can have a downside. Praised as a noble patriot by some newspapers, he was vilified and caricatured by others. The Whig grandee Charles James Fox, then briefly in power, called him *'a madman, and a dishonest one.'* Horace Walpole, every ready with the bitter word as far as Frederick was concerned, did not hold back:

'His immorality, martial pretences & profaneness covered him with odium and derision. Blasphemy was the puddle in which washed away his episcopal Protestantism… think of a reformation of parliament by admitting Roman Catholics to vote at elections! That it was sanctioned by a Protestant Bishop is not strange, he would call Musselmen (Muslims) *to the poll, were there any within the diocese of Derry.'*

Muslims being allowed to vote? The very idea! Purporting to be written by a lady of loose morals, a satirical poem in *The Volunteer Evening Post* began:

'A deadly pale o'erspreads my face / The Herveys all are such a fickle race / Odd neutral things of maggots born and bred / From soft Lord Fanny down to mitred Fred / But true the good, untrue the boded ill / I see a letter from Downhill…'

Frederick's family in England were mortified. Through civil wars and bloody power struggles, the Herveys had managed to serve every royal family for nearly 300 years and now Frederick was portrayed as having turned against the king. Bess, who through the Devonshires would have heard all the London political gossip first-hand, cringed at her association and began to called her father *'Pansey.'* The nickname did not imply homosexuality as it does today – that is a 20th century connotation – rather it was her derisory term for a free-thinker (for which the pansy flower was once a symbol).

Still, for anyone who knows Ireland, one quote from this period stands out from the rest, made by Frederick to some fellow reformers:

'Quench but this firebrand of religious discordancy… and ye will soon see the pure lambent flame of liberty cherish and enlighten Ireland. But until ye can forgive and reciprocally tolerate each other ye must expect to find yourselves ultimately tools and victims.'

If the next two centuries of Irish history could have been foretold in a line, surely it was the second one above. Frederick may have acted selfishly, but he also had a talent for hitting the nail on the head. As the poet Thomas Grey remarked of him: *'sometimes from vanity he may do the right thing.'* On the question of religious tolerance, he was very far ahead of his time. It has been said that he did not care what others thought of him, which is not entirely true, but the backlash against his political campaigning would claim one innocent victim. Some even said that it killed her.

From 'Excellent' to 'Majestic Ruin.' Elizabeth Davers, shortly after her marriage to Frederick in 1752 (above) and with little Louisa, more than twenty years later (right). After a quarrel in 1782, the couple never spoke again.

© The National Trust

Frederick's second daughter, Bess, captured by Joshua Reynolds in her mid-twenties. With typical English understatement, she was once described as 'a delightful creature, but ever so slightly naughty.'

Also by Reynolds, the naughtiest of them all; brother Augustus, the 3rd Earl of Bristol, more popularly known as 'the English Casanova.' Sent off to sea at the age of 11, the hard-bitten Augustus was Frederick's polar opposite and disliked him intensely, probably with good reason.

© The National Trust

Frederick's 'chere cousine,' Frideswide Mussenden, whose name he would tragically immortalise in his temple at Downhill. Although a wife and a mother, it can be seen from this exquisite miniature that Frideswide was barely more than a child herself.

© National Gallery of Ireland

Frederick in the garden of the Villa Borghese, Rome, with his granddaughter, Caroline (Mary's daughter), in 1790. To the modern eye, there is something slightly unsettling about this tableau, but it was by no means the most contrived artwork commissioned by Frederick and quite typical of the period. Painted by Hugh Douglas Hamilton, one of Frederick's favourite contemporary artists, it is the only original portrait of him left in Ireland. © National Gallery of Ireland

'Oh Emma, who'd ever be wise, If madness be loving of thee?'

Emma Hamilton, adopting a deceptively demure pose, painted by George Romney in her late teens. It was rumoured that she and Frederick had an affair, but they were just good friends.

© National Maritime Museum, Greenwich

The irresistible Madame Ritz, suffering a major wardrobe malfunction. The Prussian beauty was the love of Frederick's later life, but he dropped her like a hot potato when she was arrested. Pictured here in her twenties, by Anna Dorothea Therbusch. © Stiftung Preussische Schlosser und Garten Berlin – Brandenburg

How could anyone be cruel to a lovely chap like this? Frederick's youngest son, Frederick William, who was much nicer to his father than his father was to him. He became the 5th Earl of Bristol and, at huge expense, finished Ickworth House, just visible in the background. © The National Trust

'An impudent house,' according to Frederick, and 'a stupendous monument of folly,' according to his wife. Frederick never saw Ickworth House, since he left England before the foundations were laid and did not return alive. However, he had already built a smaller version, Ballyscullion, near Bellaghy in County Londonderry and although it was never finished, Frederick liked Ballyscullion so much that he decided to replicate it on a grander scale.

© The National Trust

Downhill as it is today (above) and Frederick's great west wing gallery as it looked in Edwardian times (left). We need to imagine this with an elegant painted ceiling, stuffed with antique statues, and with Frederick showing off his latest acquisitions to some charming lady friend. Or just wearing his dressing gown, since he had to traverse the gallery to reach his bedroom, through the far door.

© The National Trust

The great art patron. If Frederick looks rather severe and his room somewhat gloomy, it is because this picture was commissioned after his death. It now hangs in the entrance hall of Ickworth House.

© The National Trust

Did they, or didn't they?

In December 1783, just after Frederick returned to Downhill from the convention in Dublin, a newspaper called *The Freeman's Journal* printed a letter written under the pen-name 'Scaevola' (which means left-handed in Latin). It did not name Frederick, but it was clear that the letter was about him and it alleged that he was the lover and seducer of the married woman, Mrs. Mussenden. Frederick was outraged and Frideswide mortified; as can be imagined, her husband, Daniel, was also less than pleased. Almost immediately, a response was published in *The Volunteer Evening Post*, from 'An Inhabitant of Lisburne' (Lisburn is close to Larchfield, where Frideswide lived). That letter defended Frederick and Frideswide to the hilt, calling her *'virtuous, chaste and innocent,'* and Frederick *'the most learned scholar, the warmest friend, the most charitable prelate, the most liberal ecclesiastic, and the most humane man we have ever seen.'* It also displayed rather more familiarity with Frideswide's domestic arrangements than an average inhabitant of Lisburn might have been expected to possess, saying that she kept Frederick's portrait in her best room and that the only disagreement between Frederick and Daniel had been over a book, *Cicero's Epistles*. It pointed out that, when Frederick had been staying with Frideswide earlier that year, her father had been dying, which was true. The 'Inhabitant of Lisburne' knew so much, one must suspect that he was none other than Frideswide's brother, Harry Bruce, but there is no way to be certain.

Frederick threatened to sue *The Freeman's Journal* for libel, but didn't. Whether he was dissuaded by the Mussendens, or whether he was afraid of more information coming out, again there is no way to be certain. For example, it was not entirely true that the only disagreement between he and Daniel had been over a book. Daniel had once come across Frederick and Frideswide *'in a retired place'* and now refused to let her see him without a chaperone present. To dispel the rumours, Frederick wanted the Mussendens to visit him at

Downhill in a public display of friendship, but Daniel refused to cooperate.

So did they, or didn`t they? Was Frideswide ever more than a *'chere cousine,'* or was she just an innocent young woman, tarnished by an unfortunate association? It casts a certain light on Frederick, if one detects more in his behaviour than that of *'un bon Papa.'* Perhaps 'Scaevola' was spreading a wicked lie, but then why didn`t Frederick sue *The Freeman`s Journal* and the printer (Forbes Ross of Crane Lane, Templebar, Dublin)? He certainly had enough money to tie both paper and printer up in legal knots and probably close them down. On the other hand, although he would not go himself, Daniel did permit Frideswide to visit Frederick at Downhill, provided she was chaperoned, which hardly seems the action of an upright Presbyterian who believed himself a cuckold. Although, it can equally be argued that his insistence on a chaperone and his anger with Frederick meant that he had specific concerns.

The calm after the storm

Lord Northington, the Lord Lieutenant, had a warrant for Frederick`s arrest and was ready to act on it at a moment`s notice. He was replaced early in 1784 by the Duke of Rutland, who was even more keen to make an example of our hero. Rutland wrote that *'His Lordship`s forwardness to seize any opportunity of involving this country in disorder and tumult can be little doubted.'* Rutland`s assessment seemed justified when Frederick`s Volunteer nephew, George Robert 'the Fighting Fitzgerald,' travelled north to receive the freedom of Derry city. However, William Pitt the Younger, who was now the British first minister, advised against arresting Frederick. Pitt thought that a prosecution might make him even more popular and could even fan the flames of rebellion. Anyway, since Frederick was an establishment figure, the establishment could not put him on trial without looking ridiculous. The best possible outcome was for the whole fuss to die down and it is entirely possible that, via an emissary, Pitt had a quiet word in Frederick`s ear, reminding him of the esteem he had once had for the first minister`s father (who had died six years previously). Frederick`s passions could be sudden and intense, but they could cool just as quickly.

He did not lose interest in politics, but rather eased himself out of Volunteering and instead gave himself over to the life of a country gentleman at his beloved Downhill, which he called his *'temple of the winds.'* In 1785, *Town and Country* magazine published a lengthy article about a relationship between the 'Patriotic Prelate' and a certain 'Mrs. H.' She was supposedly the wife of a clergyman, but her full identity was never established. Living at Downhill without his family, Frederick treated the mansion as a massive bachelor pad. One wing was given over to guest accommodation and the other would eventually house Frederick`s gallery, library, study and bedroom. And whereas nowadays, we tend to socialise in restuarants, pubs and clubs, in the late 1700s such establishments were rare outside the major cities, so Georgian country houses were designed for socialising. Downhill had a wine cellar and Frederick imported his in bulk, directly from Bordeaux. Through his love of music, he befriended Denis O`Hampsey, the blind harper of Magilligan. O`Hampsey was the last exponent of an ancient Irish harp playing style and performed many concerts at Downhill for Frederick and his guests. After O`Hampsey died, his instrument was kept at the house for years and is nowadays exhibited at the Guinness distillery in Dublin.

A letter to Mary in February 1785 paints a rosy picture of Frederick`s lifestyle:

'Downhill is becoming Elegance itself – 300,000 Trees without Doors upon all the banks & all the Rocks, & almost as many pictures & Statues within Doors count very well. I have had no gout this winter which I attribute to Musick or harmony of mind. Everything is Redolent of Joy & youth & we commonly sit down to Table from 20

to 25. We have cold suppers, and a bottle of Champaign at each end of the table – the Songsters sing Ketches, & I go to Bed which just now invites.'

Town and Country magazine reinforced this image of a cultured nobleman at his ease:

'The Patriotic Prelate in private life is a most amiable character; he is friendly, hospitable, charitable and humane… our hero is neither a foxhunter or a gamester, a jockey or a Bacchanalian (all traits of the aristocracy), *yet he loves a cheerful glass as well as any man in London, or Londonderry.'*

On the subject of Mrs. H., the report continued; *'This lady is the daughter of a reputable tradesman who gave her a genteel education.'* By the time she grew to womanhood, *'she was tall and elegant in her figure, moved with peculiar grace and ease; her face was a regular oval, her eyes large, blue and enchanting, where a thousand cupids lay in ambush. When she smiled a most engaging dimple presented itself to view.'* Her marriage to the Reverend Mr. H. had been short-lived and the writer accused her of *'wearing the breeches'*. He concluded; *'In the Patriotic Prelate she has met a man after her own heart… and they now seem to go hand in hand.'*

The story did not cause a scandal, unlike the uproar over Frideswide the previous year. Nor did Frederick threaten to sue, so it must be assumed that Mrs. H. was indeed his regular and agreeable companion. Apparently she liked books, which along with her dimple and large blue eyes, would have endeared her to Frederick. Whilst he was hardly the first bishop to enjoy a mistress, such arrangements were usually closely-guarded secrets and certainly not tittle-tattle for the popular press. The *Town and Country* article shows the extent to which he had become an object of amused curiosity – a celebrity, in other words.

Since Frideswide visited Downhill during this period, it must either be believed that she never was more than a *'chere cousine,'* or that Frederick was quite a player. That he enjoyed the company of pretty women, there can be no doubt. That his brother Augustus, his father, some uncles and his son Jack were enthusiastic philanderers again is beyond doubt. Neither was his daughter Bess a retiring wallflower; besides the Devonshires, she would be romantically linked with several other important figures. However, in Frederick`s case, the evidence is less conclusive and each reader must make of it what they will.

In Ireland, all the great yarns that are still spun about 'the Earl Bishop' emanate from this period. The wing of Downhill given over to guests was laid out along the 'curate`s corridor,' so called because Frederick invited holy men of all denominations to stay for dinners and drinks. After one such feast, he suggested a walk on the spectacular beach below the house and the company, composed of a mixture of his own Church of Ireland clergy and several Presbyterian ministers, readily agreed. However, when the party reached the sands, they found grooms waiting with horses, saddled and ready to ride. Frederick demanded a race between his clergy and the Presbyterians, which the latter easily won; apparently, some portly Church of Ireland jockeys even took tumbles. Laughing, Frederick accused his clergy of being too fat and threatened to open a riding school for them.

On another occasion, when a parish had fallen vacant, Frederick invited all his hopeful curates up for another of his feasts. A standard toast at his table was *'a rot amongst the rectors,'* in anticipation of such opportunities. The invitees would have hurried to Downhill, assuming that their bishop would use the dinner to announce the new rector (who could then live comfortably for the rest of his life from tithes and rents). Instead, after a slap-up feed, Frederick again suggested a walk on the beach. This time, there were no horses, but he pointed to a faraway rock and declared that whoever could run there and back the fastest, would win the parish. Stuffed with food and probably half-drunk, the poor curates stumbled off, little realising until it was too late that they had been directed towards quicksand. Apparently, none finished the course. Another version of this story has Frederick sending them across a bog, but even a curate would need to be stupendously drunk not to recognise a bog when he saw one.

One can interpret such actions as cruelty, an accusation that had already been levelled at Frederick in relation to his family (and would be again). Or perhaps he was making an elaborate point about the yawning chasm between the lifestyle of his clergy and what they preached in church on Sundays. Perhaps he was just having a laugh; whatever his motives, it was not typical ecclesiastic behaviour. These tales are fondly recalled today, for although Ireland has long been a religious country, the appreciation of 'a character' runs deeper still. Thanks to his combination of indiscriminate charity, rebellious passions and wicked wit, Frederick was deemed an honorary Irishman. When women spent the night at Downhill, he would dismiss the servants and then sprinkle the guest corridors with flour before retiring, so as he could tell the following morning whether anyone had visited their bedrooms, during the wee small hours.

It was also said of Frederick that he sometimes went to wise women – soothsayers – but only in disguise. Certainly, in the Magilligan area beside Downhill, there was no shortage of traditional beliefs in those days. When one such woman asked him who he was, he wouldn`t answer, so she declared, *'Ah sure you are the Devil himself, or else you are the Bishop of Derry.'*

Another superstitious story has Frederick coming into possession of an iron casket, which contained the prophesies of Saint Columba, or Colum Cille, the 6th century missionary and patron saint of Derry. Legend had it that the casket could only be opened by a man who was not born of woman, who rode a horse that had not been foaled. It might be recalled that Frederick was supposedly born by Caesarian section. He apparently rode a mare that had been born the same way.

So he took the casket to the Mussenden Temple, where he managed to open it. A nest of tiny snakes erupted hissing from the box and when they touched the ground, dissolved into dust. Frederick then read the prophesies but as he did, his face turned pale and without sharing the revelations, ordered them locked away again and the casket hidden forever. The son of the stonemason who built the Mussenden Temple used to repeat this story frequently and sincerely, claiming that Frederick was so terrified by what he had seen, he had become a Papist, had never again slept in the same place for more than a few nights running, and had spent his final years scurrying around Catholic countries before dying miserably in Rome. It certainly was one explanation for the way the rest of his life would unfold.

In 1785, Frederick gave a London-based visitor directions for Downhill:

'The large yarn vessels are every day sailing from Liverpool to Derry, Coleraine & Belfast. Two days carry you from London to Liverpool in a Diligence (coach) & from thence either 36 hours or 40 will land you in the Coleraine River under my park wall. This is but a short journey to see an old friend.'

Four days to reach Downhill from London; no wonder visitors tended to stay for weeks at a time, once they finally arrived. If Frederick ever did come close to creating a slice of heaven on earth, then surely it must have been during the 1780s at Downhill. Perhaps in his letters to Mary, who was the only family member to remain on friendly terms with him at this time, he exaggerated his contentment, although letters to other correspondents also sparkle with zest. However, any letters to his wife were nothing more than the usual tart lectures about the need to economise. In 1785, Louisa, who was then 18 and still living with her mother, had a nervous breakdown, so Elizabeth took her up to London from Ickworth to try to cheer her up. By that time, the townhouse was free again and Elizabeth used it regardless of Frederick`s wishes.

Once, Jack arrived unexpectedly at Downhill with a group of friends, but was sent packing after a few nights and had to seek shelter at a neighbouring farmhouse. A version had it that the young men raided Frederick`s cellars and got rip-roaring drunk; another had Jack fighting with his father over money; yet another had Frederick throwing Jack out because he declared himself a Tory. Rowdy drinking, demands for money and a disavowal of parental values – a familiar litany to any father with a son. Frederick had never rebelled against his own father because he had never seen enough of him to do so, but Jack had obviously inherited the wild ways of his great-uncles, Tom and Harry, and of the 'English Casanova,' his uncle Augustus.

Another Harry lurks in the background; Harry Bruce, Frideswide`s brother, who was at this time attending Trinity College in Dublin. Although a penniless student, his role in Frederick`s life would soon surpass that of his sister`s, in both significance and endurance.

Tragic Frideswide

The happy days at Downhill came to an abrupt end in the spring of 1785, when Frideswide died, still only in her early twenties. It was sometimes said, by the more romantically-minded, that she died of a broken heart, never having overcome the shame of being labelled an adultress. Her cause of death is not in fact recorded. However, it is known that she did not die at her home in Larchfield, rather at Clifton, in Bristol, from which it may be deduced that she was defeated by a more prosaic, if no less painful affliction. The spring of Hotwells, which was on the bank of the River Avon beside Clifton, was destroyed in the 19th century during work to make the river more navigable. However, in the 18th century, Hotwells was almost as popular as nearby Bath for invalids seeking a cure. In particular, it was thought that the waters could combat consumption, as tuberculosis was then called. In Britain at that time, one in five deaths were caused by the disease and the spa was a destination of last resort.

It might be remembered that during his last trip abroad, Frederick had tried to buy the Temple of Vesta at Tivoli, to import it to Downhill. Now, the architect Michael Shanahan was building a version of it within view of the house, also perched on a cliff, just like the original. In the Roman pantheon, Vesta was the virgin goddess of domesticity. Perhaps with that image in mind, Frederick named his elegant little copy in memory of his *'chere cousine.'* Inside, the Mussenden Temple was a library and again it is romantic to picture Frederick and Frideswide enjoying it in happier times, reading and relaxing as the waves washed on the rocks far below. However, it was unfinished when she died and in truth, Frederick himself would never use it very much; perhaps the association was too sad.

Outside, the Latin inscription around the Temple is from the Roman poet and philosopher Lucretius, and roughly translates as:

'How delightful it is, when the winds have whipped up the waters of the great sea, to watch the perils of another from dry land.'

The quote is not meant to be taken literally. Rather than an expression of sadism, it is a metaphor for being secure in one's personal philosophy, when others are struggling to make sense of the world. Naming his temple for her, Frederick did not see the irony; so sure of his own enlightened opinions, he had brought a storm down on this young mother's head. Frideswide must have struggled to make sense of the world, when it turned against her so.

Frideswide's son, William, grew up at Larchfield and married a woman called Sarah Low. On the 25th of October 1854, at Balaclava in the Crimea, their son, also called William, would survive the charge of the Light Brigade.

At around the same time as Frideswide died, Frederick fell seriously ill. He described his treatment to Mary:

'I have this moment been rubb'd all over with Laudanum especially on the Pitt of the stomach & drench'd with Aether by my poor Physician. I conclude, tho' he does not confess it to me, that he took the disorder for the gout in the stomach and wishes to avert a return. I reckon I must pass the winter in a warmer climate.'

Laudanum is opium dissolved in alcohol and 'Aether' is ether, the flammable solvent, then used as a general anaesthetic. It is difficult to imagine the effect of being drenched by both at once, but it must have been interesting, to say the least. As soon as he was able to travel, Frederick ordered more work to be carried out at Downhill, then took himself off to Bath, where after *'various relapses,'* he reported to Mary that he was *'at length crawling to the Pump'* (the hot water spring). His treatment was augmented: *'Aether and Vitriol contribute, Hemlock & Laudanum assist, Corelli, Bach and Abel come in as powerful allies.'* Vitriol is sulphuric acid; hemlock the poisonous plant then used as a sedative; and Arcangelo Corelli, Johann Sebastian Bach and Carl Friedrich Abel are composers, a reference to the entertainments available at Bath in the evenings. Strong medicine indeed, although Frederick makes no mention on this occasion of being bled. It was common medical practice then to open a patient's veins, in order to balance what were thought to be 'humours' within the body, ususally doing much more harm than good.

After Bath, Frederick went to Bristol, his namesake city, to take the waters at Hotwells, where Frideswide had died only a few months previously. Then, true to his word, that autumn he embarked on his fourth continental journey, in search of warmer weather. The combination of Frideswide's death and his illness had perhaps led him to contemplate his own mortality, for he also decided to attempt a Hervey family reunion.

Family secrets

Frederick's idea of a reconciliation did not stretch as far as his estranged wife, but he picked up Frederick William, who was now 16 years old, and headed for France. He met Mary and her daughter Caroline, then 7 years old, in Lyons. Not feeling strong enough to tackle the Alps, Frederick instead made for the Riviera and crossed into Italy by hugging the coast. His reputation was now such that news of his movements travelled faster than he did and at the start of 1786, the Roman grapevine positively shook when it was heard that *il Vescovo Inglese,* as he was known there, was on his way. The touring English nobility anticipated his arrival with curiosity, whilst the artistic community was looking forward to having its coffers replenished. Neither would be disappointed.

However, one Englishwoman in Rome dreaded the arrival of *Pansey*. Bess had been in Italy since the previous year, under extraordinary circumstances. Pregnant by the Duke of Devonshire, she had enlisted her brother Jack's help in fleeing abroad to give birth to the child. Neither Bess nor the Duke wanted the Duchess, Georgiana, to find about their liaison, let alone Bess's family or anyone else for that matter. Jack, who at this stage was throwing himself at practically every woman he met, had set out with Bess and his own wife, the long-suffering Elizabeth Drummond, who surely must have regretted ever having heard of the Herveys. The couple even brought their little daughter, Eliza, then 6 years old.

Wearing loose clothes to disguise her condition, Bess, accompanied by Jack, a maid and a servant called Louis, took a detour to Ischia, the volcanic island at the northern end of the Bay of Naples. Bess intended to give birth there and Jack returned to his wife and child in Naples. She settled down to wait and even received a letter from the Devonshires. Referring to her gambling and to a fling she herself had had with the politician Charles James Fox ('the Eyebrow'), which Bess knew about but the Duke didn't, Georgiana wrote: *'I think I have got out of all my messes. The Eyebrow is going & I have left off my playing & extravagance – in short I hope Canis* (the Duke) *will tell you that your Rat* (Georgiana) *is not very naughty. As for Canis he is the best of Dogs… Oh Bess you must come very soon & make your Dog and Rat happy.'* An addendum by the Duke hoped *'you are not out of humour with, or forgetfull of Canis, who loves you as much if more than ever.'* With his illegitimate child due any day, one can imagine Bess`s feelings on reading this.

Then she learned that other English tourists were on their way to Ischia and feared discovery. She sent for Jack, who during a storm took her in an open boat around to Salerno, the next city down the coast from Naples, and directed her and Louis to a brothel in the harbourside village of Vietri, with Louis now in on the secret and pretending to be her husband. After a fortnight confined there, at the height of the August heat, she gave birth to a baby girl, Caro, who just six days later was handed over to foster parents of Jack`s acquaintance in Naples. Jack certainly knew his way around these Italian ports. In the meantime, notwithstanding the presence of his wife and daughter, he had started a separate intrigue of his own, pursuing a married princess called Roccafionta. But the best was yet to come; to explain Bess`s three-week disappearance, she and Jack put it about that she had been shipwrecked and incredibly, everyone believed them.

Bess had returned to Naples and was visiting her baby daughter covertly, whilst otherwise pretending that nothing untoward had happened (apart, of course, from the shipwreck). However, she was terrified that her secret would be uncovered. The closer that Frederick now drew to Rome, the more she felt like a guilty daughter. His proposed reconciliation was timed for Easter week, 1786. Mary and young Frederick William were already with their father; Bess and Jack were summoned for what she called *'a trial of Pansey`s feelings towards us all.'*

The reunion not so much a trial of Frederick`s feelings as an unmitigated disaster. Bess thought that her father was behaving strangely, which he may have been, apparently more interested in art than in his children. Perhaps there were echoes now of Frederick`s own father, who had ignored his children completely, or perhaps he was disguising insecurity with indifference. Still, given the scale of the cover-up that Bess and Jack were engaged in, it could hardly be said that all the Hervey children were behaving normally either. Jack had not spoken to his father since being turfed out of Downhill and now Bess tried to make peace between them, but was unable to. The subject of money reared its head; Jack was running up huge debts in Naples, but once again Frederick refused to help him out. The British consul in Florence wrote to his friend Horace Walpole, knowing how much he disliked Frederick:

'He moves from place to place to avoid his eldest son whom he leaves in absolute (financial) *distress, at a time when he himself squanders vast sums in what he calls the Beaux Arts, though he only purchases the dregs of them.'*

To make matters worse, Bess thought Mary was jealous of her, which she probably was, but also, Bess`s status as the Devonshire`s 'companion' was an ongoing source of society gossip and the relatively strait-laced Mary disapproved. Frederick indeed left Rome to avoid Jack, fleeing to Naples of all places, where he fell seriously ill again. Word spread quickly and soon, the vultures were circling. In August 1786, the Earl of Tyrone wrote to the Duke of Rutland, who was still Lord Lieutenant of Ireland:

'I have an account that the Bishop of Derry is in a wretched & emaciated state, & that we shall hear of his death in a very short while. Let me mention to you that the transference of my brother the Bishop of Ossory to the see of Derry is an object which on many counts I have greatly at heart…'

Jack returned to Naples, whereupon Frederick fled north to Florence then Cento, so Jack gave up the pursuit of his father`s money and renewed his pursuit of Princess Roccafionta. Feeling sorry for Jack`s wife and daughter, Mary invited them to accompany her to Switzerland. She now received enough money from both Lord Erne and from her father to live modestly, but well. Then, as Frederick struggled to recover, he received some shocking news from Ireland; his nephew, George Robert 'the Fighting Fitzgerald,' had been hanged for murder.

It might be remembered that 'the Fighting Fitzgerald' had been at Frederick's side during the drama of the Volunteer convention in Dublin two years previously and had subsequently been granted the freedom of Derry. In his home county of Mayo, he was less well-regarded. Perhaps Jack should have tried the following methods to extract money from Frederick; when George Robert's rascally father had refused to hand over an inheritance, his swashbuckling son had chained him to his pet bear. When that hadn't worked, he had chained him to a horse and when that hadn't worked, the old man had found himself chained up in a cave. Another version of this story has the son chaining his father inside the cave and guarding the entrance with his bear for fifteen months, which seems less likely but given the levels of lunacy at work, not impossible. George Robert had been duly arrested, but had escaped and kidnapped his father again and had him imprisoned him on an island off Sligo. He also set up some cannon in an old ring fort on his father's estate, where he holed up with his gang of lackeys. Incredibly, for most of this period, George Robert was a magistrate; if this was how the law behaved, one can only imagine what the outlaws were like. The end had come during yet another quarrel where George Robert had had three men kidnapped, who were then shot whilst trying to escape. The County Sherriff was an enemy and had ordered 'the Fighting Fitzgerald' hanged. The Fitzgeralds were landed gentry, so it was rather surprising that the sentence actually went ahead. The rope had broken on the first attempt, had been too long on the second and finally worked on the third. It is said that George Robert's daughter, who even before his death lived with foster parents in Dublin, was protected from hearing of her father's fate until one day eight years later, when she read of it in a newspaper which she found on top of a wardrobe. She then died of shock.

Frederick deteriorated on hearing the news. Bess headed for Venice, where she hoped to meet the Devonshires, and stopped at Cento on the way, but Frederick was in bed *'saying he is dying, seeing no body but Frederick* (Frederick William), *yet very likely issuing forth some of his terrible letters to my Mother… I never was so distrest.'*

A verdant plain

Frederick recovered during the autumn and, the weather notwithstanding, was back in Downhill by the winter of 1786-87. The aftermath of the botched reunion still reverberated as he now fell out with Frederick William, over his youngest son's refusal to travel to the Netherlands with a tutor, as Frederick wanted him to. At that point, the Netherlands were in a state of violent revolt, in a foretaste of the storm that would hit France two years later. Understandably, Elizabeth did not want Frederick William to go and Frederick was angry with his son for listening to his mother. On good terms with Mary alone, he also complained about Bess and Louisa being interested only in his money:

'I strike against my heart and it hurts my hand, all but a corner of it which will not petrify – in the meantime I am stoick enough to find adopted children, brothers, everything, & can smile with ineffable contempt at the injuries and revilements I incur: in this country I am more popular & more courted than ever: yet I do nothing but build houses, plant forests, decorate villas, &c. & live with my acquaintance as my inclination induces & my property prescribes.'

Whilst it is not certain who *'my acquaintance'* was (the mysterious Mrs. H., perhaps?), translated, he was saying that he was the one with the money, so everyone else could take a running jump. Although he was obviously hurt by his isolation, largely it was his own fault. Nor was his heart as petrified as he pretended; working behind the scenes, in 1787 he helped Jack to procure the post of British minister to the court of Tuscany. The region was then an independent Grand Duchy with Florence as its capital, another Italian city which Frederick adored.

One of the *'adopted children'* he had in mind was Henry Hervey Bruce, or Harry. Frideswide`s eldest brother had graduated from Trinity College and was about to be ordained into the Church of Ireland; he was also 23 years old, dirt poor and in love. The object of his affection was one Letitia Barnard, a granddaughter of the Bishop Barnard who had vacated Derry for Frederick. Her parents were friends of Frederick`s, which shows that Harry must have been in Frederick`s orbit during all this time.

Since he had no money or prospects, the Barnards would not accept Harry, a predicament which meant that *'two innocent bosoms were resigned to the horrid tyranny of despair.'* The situation of a novice clergyman courting against familial wishes must have reminded Frederick of his younger self. He promised Harry the next vacant parish in Derry, which turned out to be Tamlaghtfinlagan, centred on the village of Ballykelly. He also gave him £400 per year from his own pocket. Thus reassured, the Barnards allowed the lovers to marry. Later, Frederick would write to Harry about Letitia:

'She was your first parish. Ballykelly is at best but a lawful concubine & very secondary to your true legitimate & carnal wife for you were a man before you became a Parson & therefore conjugal duties are prior to clerical ones.'

Strange words for a bishop, but it shows how close the two men were. Harry was extremely grateful to his patron and would now become Frederick`s trusted agent, taking on many duties beyond his role as rector of Tamlaghtfinlagan. His loyalty was absolute and eventually, would be lavishly rewarded, even beyond the bestowal of a wife, a job and the handsome church in Ballykelly that Frederick also co-funded and which is still in use to this day.

Downhill was expanding all the time, to receive the art treasures flooding in from the continent. Still, there is only so much treasure a mansion can hold, so Frederick decided to build another one, as different from Downhill as it was possible to imagine. During his travels in England, he had visited a house called Belle Isle, set on an island in Lake Windermere. The Lake District was then becoming fashionable and Belle Isle is quite unusual (it still exists). Oval in shape and with a domed roof, outwardly it is modelled on the Pantheon, the Roman rotunda and architectural marvel admired by all neoclassicists. Design-wise, Downhill is a mish-mash of inputs from a range of sources, but Frederick`s vision for Ballyscullion, as his new piece of heaven on earth would be called, was both unique and his own. From a central rotunda, two colonnades would curve outward, ending in gallery pavillions where he could exhibit his burgeoning art collection. At a time when paintings were displayed willy-nilly, he had the idea of hanging them in schools, which nowadays seems perfectly logical, but Frederick was one of the first to suggest doing so. And whereas Downhill`s setting was wild and sublime, Ballyscullion`s would be gentle and pastoral, in the more sheltered and fertile south of County Derry. He described the site to his favourite daughter:

'Imagine to yourself then my dear Mary a globular hillock of gravel carpetted with dry green grass whose declivity reaches at the end of half a mile to the Banks of the River Bann or rather of Lough Beg, the small lake… an immense ridge of the Conical Mountains of Mourne – such is my Prospect to the South. On the East, which is the aspect of my Eating Room, the River Bann & the hills of the county of Antrim, together with a few hundred acres of my own estate, & a bridge which I am on the point of building will serve to amuse our eyes when we are not employing our knives and forks.'

Like the Mussenden Temple, Ballyscullion would also have a Latin inscription around its rotunda, adapted from Virgil and translating as:

'Here is a verdant plain; I will place a temple of marble beside the waters, where the vast Bann strays in sluggish windings, and clothes his banks with tender reeds.'

Reinvigorated by his new building project and its verdant plain, Frederick did not hang around for very long to contemplate either. By 1788 he was on the move again and the autumn of that year found him in France, then on the verge of massive, bloody change.

A nation of baboons

France had suffered from several years of poor grain harvests and had burdened itself with enormous debt, fighting England in North America. The country was also an administrative mess, with chaotic government and inadequate roads, which hindered trade and made it hard to get much-needed food to the cities. A malnourished populace was in a dangerous state of unrest, not that the nobility seemed to notice or care. Frederick himself witnessed the *'Ancien Regime'* at play in the royal hunting grounds at Chantilly, north of Paris, just months before the end came:

'Previous to the Chace (hunt)*… they all met under a superb tent, with the Princess of Monaco the Queen of the feast – here they devour'd a most comfortable and regular dinner of Three courses and a Desert, followed with coffee and liqueurs and thus with a Body cramm'd & vacant mind they hied them to the chace, which to the poor stag lasted two hours. (They) were dress'd like so many drummers & trumpeters in a Peach Color'd Cloth, coat, waistcoat & Breeches lac'd down the seams with silver – their hair as completely dress'd as if going to a Ball, & their Jack boots the only emblem of hunting.'*

Not so much a case of 'let them eat cake,' as let them drink coffee and liqueurs. Frederick made for Bordeaux, intending to continue south into Spain, but he abandoned that plan when he heard how bad the inns were and instead wandered around the south of France until the summer of 1789. Perhaps there was something in that myth about him opening the box of prophesies, for as long as he kept moving, he remained healthy: *'the high road is my Apothecary's shop & my Horse my medicine.'* France was disintegrating around him, but the constant change of scenery kept him in good spirits. Just three weeks before the storming of the Bastille, he wrote:

'This Frippery Country is still the same, a skipping dancing tribe – they are fit only for themselves – and when the circling glass goes round they talk of Beauties which they never saw, & Fancy raptures which they never felt – all now is commotion, & soon will be singsong, in the meantime the hot heads let one another's blood, the Clergy arise against he Bishops, & the laity against the Nobles.'

Frederick lifts a quote here from a popular 18th-century stage tragedy; he certainly foresaw tragedy, but not the sheer scale of it. As the historian Alexis de Tocqueville later said of the French Revolution: *'Never was any such event so inevitable, yet so completely unforeseen.'* In the next few years, King Louis XVI and his Austrian queen, Marie Antoinette, would be held prisoner then guillotined and tens of thousands of nobles and ordinary citizens would be executed in the Reign of Terror (quite likely including the liqueur-quaffing, peach-coated hunters whom Frederick had observed at Chantilly, for the royal castle there would be destroyed). Hundreds of thousands would die as France descended into famine and civil war and the death toll would climb into the millions as the Revolutionary Armies took on Austria, Prussia, Britain, the Italian states and Spain. A minor Corsican nobleman`s son of Italian extraction, christened Napoleone di Buonaparte, would rise through the chaos to dominate the early decades of the following century.

The French establishment had supported the American revolutionaries of the New World, without anticipating that their ideals might infect the old one. Similarly, many English Whig liberals like Frederick were appalled when the rights of man were so vehemently asserted closer to home. The bloodthirsty language about overthrowing tyrants which he himself had used in Ireland was now common currency in France, but Frederick suddenly became quite the counter-revolutionary, dismissing the French as a *'nation of Baboons'* and *'a band of Monkeys who have burst into a shop of old China and are breaking all about them'* (which at least shows that the modern-day insult of 'cheese-eating surrender monkeys' is not entirely new).

Frederick did not know it, but with her matchless talent for placing herself at the centre of high drama, at this pivotal point in history his daughter Bess was actually in the French king`s palace of Versailles, with the Devonshires. She met Marie Antionette and wished her well, and was there the first night that a mob dared to climb the gates. As Paris erupted, she even attended the theatre and the opera, before it occurred to the Duke that it might be a good idea to move his menage on to Brussels. They left just before the Bastille fell.

The vagabond star

Frederick himself headed for Pyrmont in Germany that summer, where the cream of European society carried on absolutely as normal, taking the waters by day and enjoying concerts, salons and suppers in the evenings. This, in spite of the dispossessed French aristocrats who now arrived almost daily, telling first-hand tales of horror. The French Revolution would change Europe forever, as both its ideals and violence spread, but at this precise moment, Frederick`s abiding interest was in a pagoda that he wanted to model for Ballyscullion. Perhaps he had lost his eye for the bigger picture, or perhaps some pictures are just to big to contemplate. Only later did it occur to him that what was happening in France might also happen in Ireland.

Meandering south again towards Italy, he described himself as *'a vagabond star,'* meaning a celestial body without a fixed orbit, but he may just as well have meant a 'star' in the modern, celebrity sense. With his entourage of flunkeys and travelling companions, he was feted wherever he went; the Germans in particular were very curious about this famous bishop who behaved nothing like a bishop. He was nearly 60, but said he felt 35 years younger. Travel for its own sake had become his greatest pleasure and heaven was to be found on the open road, rather than in treasure-filled mansions and in the arms of blue-eyed mistresses (although Frederick was far from finished with art, architecture and gorgeous women).

'So tomorrow we decamp, bag & baggage, & no bad baggage is mine; geese, turkeys, ducks, shoulders and legs of mutton alternately, preceded by two graduate cooks, masters of arts, who arrive just one hour before us – as much as needed to find our dinner as ready as our appetites. Lo here is our diary – At seven, help Hyperion (the sun) *to his horse, and then mount our own; trot away 15 or 18 miles without thinking about it – find excellent coffee and better cream, & two eggs ready for a rapacious stomach with all its gastric juices afloat ready to consume whatever it receives… After two hours rest, but not of our tongues, for we babble like starlings – on horseback anew, & even so we despatch 15 or 18 miles more through this ocean of sand – with now and then a village to make the remaining solitude more sensible; at close of day we close our labors & then here is our recompense: Soupe, Bouilli of duck or goose, Mutton shoulder or leg, and a large bowl of punch in which we bury all fatigue, all thought & then, as the clock strikes eight, enter the warming pan and all night asleep in Elysium* (heaven) *without one single ghost in our dreams.'*

In contrast, a less complimentary observer of Frederick`s wanderings wrote:

'With a rather numerous retinue he travels by short stages, but his horses in this sort of caravan were wretched jades and his carriage resembled the cart of a quack doctor.'

The portrait of Frederick on the rear cover of this book dates from this time. When he arrived at Naples in 1790, he met Elisabeth Vigee le Brun, then Europe`s most famous female artist. As a former portrait painter to Marie Antionette, she was now on the run from the revolution. Still in her thirties, she was also very good-looking, which may explain why Frederick is smiling. With Vesuvius in the background and a classical column at his shoulder, two of his grand obsessions are symbolised, but his amused expression and relaxed pose imply that his greatest achievement is himself. He really is the landless, younger son and commoner curate who made lucky leaps – and he knows it. As well as his own image, he commissioned a pretty self-portrait from Vigee le Brun; both now hang at Ickworth. He also met up with Mary and little Caroline in Rome; another self-satisfied but more contrived portrait from this time can be seen in the illustrations.

However, not everyone loved Frederick as much as Frederick did. On his way home to Ireland, he stopped at St James`s Palace in London to pay homage to King George III. *The Dublin Evening Post* described their encounter thus:

'On soliciting a favour from the greatest personage, instead of receiving a gracious answer, that personage turned short on his heel without deigning to make him any reply.'

The king had obviously neither forgotten nor forgiven Frederick`s political agitation in Ireland and probably felt personally aggrieved, since he had granted Derry to Frederick in the first place. Also by now, the monarch had begun to suffer from his famous bouts of madness. The snub did not go unremarked by Frederick`s social peers; periodically, he would spend the next decade trying to ingratiate himself with various political power brokers, writing long letters and communicating what he thought were clever schemes and choice pieces of intelligence. Even though one daughter – Bess – lived with the influential Devonshires and another – Louisa – would marry a future prime minister, he was never taken seriously. The British establishment considered him an outcast, and if anything, Bess and Louisa were embarrassed by their association.

Still, there was one place where Frederick could do no wrong and that was Derry. Absence really must make the heart grow fonder, because when he finally returned to the city on the 30th of November, 1790, he was met with an all-out civic celebration. An additional source of public joy might well have been Frederick`s long-promised bridge (proposed over twenty years previously), which was finally taking shape courtesy of one Lemuel Cox, a master bridge-builder from Dorchester, near Boston. Cox used oak beams shipped in from Maine and would go on to conquer rivers at Waterford, Wexford, New Ross and Portumna. Frederick`s bridge cost £16,594 and would stand for over 70 years, when it was replaced with a cast-iron one. His arrival in Derry was described in *The Dublin Evening Post:*

'About 3 o`clock in the afternoon of that day his Lordship arrived at the Waterside, and was received on the Bridge by the Corporation, citizens, and Volunteers of Derry, when a procession was formed to the Episcopal Palace where the Bishop was presented with the addresses (speeches) *of the two former bodies; after which his Lordship and all the gentlemen came to the steps in front of the Palace, and there Captain Fergusson read the address of the of the Londonderry Volunteers, in presence of the Company, under arms, and an immense multitude of spectators. When his Lordship had delivered his elegant and most animated answer, the Volunteers fired three volleys, accompanied by the loud and repeated acclamations of the populace.'*

In his speech, Frederick proclaimed that for a bishop '*The softest down in his pillow is the love of his fellow citizens, and their applause the brightest jewel in his mitre.*' However, he must have bored quite quickly of the soft down and the bright jewel, because within weeks, *The Dublin Evening Post* was able to report that:

'On Tuesday previous to Christmas day the Earl of Bristol set off from Derry on his return to the Castle of Bellaghy (Ballyscullion) *after displaying in that city several new and striking instances of princely munificence. It is impossible to describe the regret that was visible on the countenance of every citizen at his Lordship`s departure.'*

He spent Christmas at Ballyscullion and the spring and summer of 1791 moving restlessly between his rotunda there and Downhill and Derry. Verdant Ballyscullion was filled with paintings and furniture, but remained unfinished. Downhill was as sublime as ever, the great mansion finally complete after fifteen years and packed to overflowing with artworks. However, as Frederick contemplated his little temple on its cliff, who knows what feelings it now evoked? They paid him rents and tithes, which he in turn lavished on art and architecture for his private enjoyment and long periods of foreign travel, but the people of Derry still worshipped him. However, whatever it was that their bishop wanted, it was not to be found in his diocese.

In a letter that May to his old school chum William Hamilton, who had returned to England to marry for the second time, Frederick begged him to come to Ireland, but Hamilton didn`t bother. None of his children were in Ireland and he was estranged from all except Mary anyway; it is not known what became of Mrs H., but he did not seem to have any regular female company at this point either. For poor Elizabeth at Ickworth, he had only contempt, calling her *'the Majestic Ruin,'* and sending her mean-spirited letters. In Ireland, he enjoyed grand houses and public adoration, but he was lonely. By that autumn, he was on the road again and this time, would never find his way back.

A last will and testament

Annan is a small coastal town on Scotland's Solway Firth, just west of Gretna. Even today, its main feature is a red sandstone high street, characteristic of the area. In Frederick's day, there could not have been much else to Annan, yet this was where he chose to draw up his last will and testament. Suffering from gout, but perhaps more alarmingly, from a terrible depression, it was as if he had crossed from Ireland to Portpatrick (near Stranraer) and limped a few miles along the road to England, before collapsing. How much of his affliction was bodily and how much of it was in his head, is hard to say; he certainly believed himself close to death, because on the 17th of September 1791, he summoned an attorney and dictated his last wishes. In doing so, it was as if he wanted to sever all connection with his adopted country, for every last shred of his Irish property *'together with all furniture, plate, Pictures, Statues, Busts, Books &c. &c.,'* he now bequeathed to his distant cousin, Harry Bruce. He even *'interdicted all Irish letters during the weak state of my nerves.'* He did not want to hear from Ireland at all. Perhaps his disenchantment was personal; perhaps it was rooted in finding the country as hopelessly divided as ever. Sectarian gangs, particularly in Ulster, attacked landlords and one another. However, Frederick did make a provision that was typical of his character; he stipulated that Catholics living near Downhill be allowed to hold a service every Sunday in the Mussenden Temple, in the actual Temple itself and not just in its much less salubrious basement, as is more often recounted. He even laid aside a payment of £10 a year for the priest and decreed that he and his horse should be fed. This arrangement persisted until the 1850s, although a row over a missing book caused a priest to take his congregation into the basement, which was never Frederick's intention.

A noble gesture, but what a contrast to the sunny portrait painted in Naples, just a year previously. Perhaps his father's lonely, disillusioned death now haunted Frederick. His will was like a punishment for those who had deserted him. It has sometimes been suggested that Harry's immense reward was connected to a guilt felt by Frederick over Frideswide, but the truth was that Harry had been a hard-working and obedient steward and unquestioning loyalty was the trait that Frederick now most valued. In the same way that his brother Augustus had left him nothing but the entailed Bristol estates in England (although these were enormous), he did not bequeath his heir apparent, Jack, anything more than he was legally obliged to. Mary and Bess received £6,000 to divide between them, the remnants of a sum bequeathed by brother George. Also:

'I give my affectionate and dutiful daughter Lady Louisa Hervey five thousand pounds and to my undutiful and ungrateful son Frederick William Hervey I give one thousand pounds.'

Poor Frederick William; it might be remembered that he had been very dutiful indeed, tending to Frederick during his illness at Cento five years previously, but his sensible reluctance to continue his education in the Netherlands, in the middle of the Dutch Patriot Revolution, had earned his father's displeasure. By early October, Frederick had recovered sufficiently to write to Harry Bruce, informing him of his incredible good fortune, which – when one considers it – was not unlike the great leap that Frederick himself had made. He was still feeling sorry for himself:

'If I acquire strength 'tis very slowly, & the gout which at present is in both my feet scarce allows me to walk, & the bed is too debilitating to be confined to it. My Physician is a man of Ingenuity & tenderness, visits me twice a week from Dumfries & remains with me about a day and a half; his conversation is the best medicine he gives me.'

The canny doctor from Dumfries plainly saw that what his patient needed more than anything was a bit of cheering up. His treatment worked, for soon Frederick was wending his way south again. He stopped for a cure at Bath, before reaching Plymouth in January 1792, where he intended to embark for the continent. However, because of the trouble in France, sailings were irregular and in the balmy southern English sea air, one day drifted into another. The bustle of the sea port seemed to satisfy Frederick`s thirst for novelty and as he rested there, his spirits lifted. He started reading again and particularly enjoyed a book by Charles Darwin`s grandfather, Erasmus Darwin, called *The Loves of the Plants.* He answered no fewer than 93 letters, which had piled up during his dark spell. In one, he even outlined plans for having spires built within view of Ballyscullion, which showed that he was thinking positively about Ireland once again. He helped *'two miserable French exiles,'* one of them a bishop, to find accommodation and visited an eminent Greek scholar called the Reverend John Whitaker, near Truro in Cornwall. Whitaker wrote of Frederick:

'We have had a singular character with us, the Bishop of Derry. He is ingenious, lively, and a man of great taste in sculpture, painting and architecture. He came… professedly to spend two days in talking Greek to me.'

Whitaker was a very upright soul and had occasion to slap Frederick on the knee, presumably for some levity in relation to religion, although it was not unknown by now for Frederick to openly insult the king in casual conversation; the royal snub of 1790 obviously still stung. In another, more tiresome setback, he had to sack his servant, one Thomas Booth, for swindling him of money whilst settling bills at a number of inns. This was a common enough practice, whereby the innkeeper and a servant would split a mark-up on a guest too wealthy to count the pennies. Frederick must have counted the pennies and one of the offending innkeepers even paid him back.

'I am now without a single servant of confidence – I, who am made for Confidence – born confident, & who wish to trust and be trusted.'

This dilemma presaged the years to come, when more and more, he would come to rely on servants who fleeced him behind his back; people with money often find that there is no-one they can trust. He gave Mary an allowance for a coach and horses (which was more than he allowed poor Elizabeth), but held forth about the need for exercise:

'In spite of your coach, remember how very necessary exercise & open air is to a child of Caroline's age & sex – that movement, movement, is above all things essential to the human frame, which for want of it must be loaded with obstructions, bad secretions, redundant bile, & the inevitable consequences of all, bad humour, discontent, pining &c. &c.'

Perhaps he did not follow his own advice, for in May 1792, he travelled up to London to stay at St James's Square, where he fell ill with gout again. His attacks were becoming more frequent.

An impudent house

Even lying sick in London and in a permanent huff with his wife, Frederick must have had some way of knowing her movements, because that summer, he waited until she took herself off for a seaside holiday in Ramsgate, then sneaked up to Ickworth. He had not set foot in his own hereditary estate since his fight with Elizabeth ten years previously, but now he had a plan of the sort that only a hyperactive mind like his could conceive; he had decided to build yet another house. His schemes for houses were always surprising, Downhill for its location and Ballyscullion for its design. Although Ickworth Park had been crying out for a mansion since his grandfather's time, Frederick had always thought it unhealthy to live there. As the writer Arthur Young remarked:

'This eccentric man built in Ireland a large and very expensive house (Ballyscullion) *on a plan as singular as himself, and, what was more extraordinary, a repetition of it at Ickworth. But the most extraordinary circumstance was that he began it while he disliked the*

spot from the wetness of the soil, and would often tell me that he would never be such a fool as to build in so wet a situation.'

Ickworth would indeed be a repetition of Ballyscullion, with the same central rotunda, curving colonnades and gallery pavillions, but on an even grander scale. The façade of Ballyscullion was 350 feet long; Ickworth`s is almost 600. Frederick described it as *'an impudent house,'* which it certainly is, just like its builder. When Elizabeth learned of the plan, which could hardly be concealed from her since she lived less than half a mile away in Ickworth Lodge (which incidentally still stands to this day), she called the house *'a stupendous monument of folly.'* Nonetheless, over the next few years, Frederick would engage architects, including Francis Sandys who had worked on Ballyscullion, and the massive foundations would be laid by 1795.

What was he thinking of? Did he really see himself living in grandeur in a bold rotunda, with his estranged wife of forty years as his nearest neighbour, especially after all those lectures about the need to economise? Perhaps he imagined that she might dutifully look after him in his old age, or was this his way of rubbing her nose in the dirt? Perhaps he did not care what Elizabeth thought; perhaps Ickworth was a delayed reaction to growing instability in Ireland, a realisation that one day, he would have to move home. Perhaps he simply wanted to move home, as people sometimes do in their sunset years. Another possibility is, having crammed two mansions with artwork, he could not wait to finish the second before starting on a third. Since luck had gifted him his fortune, Frederick had become a collector, but more and more, the collector enjoys the thrill of the acquisition, after which he bores of the object, adds it to his pile, and starts chasing the next fix. It must not be forgotten that by now, Frederick`s income was such that he could almost have bought two Buckingham Houses a year. Since it was hardly being spent on his family, all that money had to go somewhere.

Vile animals

Having laid plans for his impudent house, Frederick set off for the continent again. He did know it, but this would be his longest trip abroad and also his last. He was accompanied by his chaplain, one Reverend Trefusis Lovell, who was rector of the Derry parish of Aghadowey. Temperamentally, Lovell seems to have been Frederick's opposite, as one would expect of an Aghadowey clergyman; prim and quiet, where his bishop was spirited and brash. They avoided France, which was now at the grim height of the Terror, and instead made their way to Germany, where they based themselves at Pyrmont. The spa town was, as ever, full of assorted European aristocrats seeking a cure, not just for their medical ailments, but their political ones, for many of them hoped that Prussia would crush revolutionary France. Frederick travelled around, admiring buildings and art galleries, whilst being admired in return by the Germans – all except for one.

Johann Wolfgang von Goethe, now mainly remembered simply by his surname, was the great genius of German literature. Also a philosopher and a scientist, he possessed a powerful intellect and was hardly the type to suffer fools gladly. Arriving at Jena, the university town in central Germany, Frederick as usual sought out the great and the good in the surrounding area and invited Goethe to visit his lodgings. According to Goethe's account, Frederick instantly attacked him over *The Sorrows of Young Werther*, the romantic novel that had made Goethe famous and in which the hero commits suicide. *Werther* had provoked a wave of copycat suicides by young men imitating the protagonist. When Frederick opened their conversation by calling it *'a completely immoral, damnable book,'* Goethe launched back at him over the evils of religion:

'What about your sermons on the terrors of hell, which so frighten the feeble spirits in your congregations that they lose their wits and end their miserable little lives in a mad house? Or your orthodox dogmas,

many of them untenable by any rational man… and yet you call a writer to account and condemn a book which, owing to the misinterpretations put upon it by a few shallow minds, has at most rid the world of a dozen fools and idlers who had nothing better to do than blow the feeble remnants of their confused little brains out altogether!'

Goethe`s account continues: *'This outburst worked on my bishop like a charm. He turned as meek as a lamb and treated me from then on, during the rest of our conversation, with the utmost courtesy and subtlest tact. Thus I passed an extremely pleasant evening with him.'* Apparently when Lovell was seeing Goethe to the door, out of Frederick`s earshot, the chaplain congratulated the writer on his tirade. Unable to stand up to Frederick himself, Lovell derived a sneaky glee when others did. However, perhaps Frederick had a point, because later in life, Goethe would distance himself from *Werther*, which he had written at the age of 24. Besides amusement, the encounter also provoked a detailed description of Frederick in his early sixties, which Goethe committed to paper the following morning:

'Of middle or rather low stature, of slight frame and countenance, lively in carriage and manners, quick in his speech, blunt, and sometimes even rude; in more than one respect narrow and one-sided, as a Briton, unbending; as an individual, obstinate; as a divine, stiff; as a scholar, pedantic. Honesty, zeal for the Good, and the unfailing results thereof, show everywhere through the disagreeable points of the above qualities, and they are balanced, too, by his extensive knowledge of the world, of men and of books, by the liberality of a noble and by the ease of a rich man. However vehemently he may be speaking (and he spares neither general nor particular circumstances) he yet listens most attentively to everything that is spoken, be it for or against him; he soon yields, if he be contradicated; contradicts if he does not like an argument, though made in his favour; now drops one sentence, now takes up another, while arguing throughout from a few chief ideas. As for the rest, his

manners seem careless, but agreeable, courtly and affable. Such is about the character of this remarkable man (for and against whom I have heard so much) as I met and observed him one evening.'

Frederick spent the better part of a year wandering through Germany, before reaching northern Italy in the autumn of 1793. It might have been expected that he would visit Florence, where his eldest son, Jack, was the British ambassador. However, now in his mid-thirties, diplomacy had not proven a brilliant career choice for Jack, since he did not have a diplomatic bone in his body. He was still a wild womaniser; finally chased away from Princess Roccafionta in Naples, he was living openly with one Lady Ann Hatton, although still married to Elizabeth Drummond. He had even tried to fight a duel with Prince Augustus, one of King George III`s sons, over the affections of this delicate flower and only the intervention of Frederick`s old school chum, Sir William Hamilton, the veteran envoy to Naples, had prevented much greater embarrassment. He was making a nuisance of himself around the Tuscan court, then most undiplomatically, called the Grand Duke a fool and his chief minister a knave. London had no choice but to recall him; when his mother heard, she managed to have his younger brother, Frederick William, appointed to travel to Florence with the bad news.

Enraged, Jack sought consolation in the company of one Elizabeth Vassall, Lady Webster, who was then separated from Lord Webster and holidaying abroad in search of wealthy male company. She wrote of Jack: *'Lord Hervey lives a good deal with me. He seems to dislike his recall and talks of going into the Navy, where by the way he is very unpopular.'* Jack soon made himself unpopular with Lady Webster, when he tried to seduce her in her carriage then begged her not to tell his wife. *'Oh! What vile animals men are,'* she wailed, *'with headstrong passions!'* She fled to Florence and Jack eventually crawled back to the Navy.

Frederick William, meanwhile, had been persuaded by his mother to seek out Frederick, as a second leg of his mission. She was very short of money and probably hoped for a reconciliation, if not for herself, then at least for poor Frederick William, who seemed to have a lot heaped on his shoulders at a young age – he was still only in his early twenties. However, his father had obviously learned of Jack`s disgrace and avoided both Florence and his youngest son, until the latter gave up his search and returned to England.

The actress and the bishop

Frederick stayed hidden until early 1794, when he turned up at the northern Italian port of Trieste, where he fell ill for a while and busied himself by writing to Sir William Hamilton in Naples, reporting on the movement of ships. The French revolutionary armies were moving south and, in his contempt for them, Frederick now acted as an amateur spy, passing on information that he thought might be of military interest. With his constant travel, he was often aware of events before the British authorities were, but his espionage was entirely freelance and how seriously it was taken, is hard to say.

He was in the habit of ending his letters to Hamilton with phrases like; *'my best love to dearest Emma.'* This was a reference to Hamilton`s second wife, Emma Hamilton, previously Emma Hart, previously Amy Lyon. Emma would later achieve notoriety as Horatio Nelson`s mistress, a status she enjoyed with the approval of her husband, who was the same age as Frederick. As 1794 wore on, Frederick became quite smitten by Emma and there were even rumours of an affair, which were untrue. Many years later, when some of Emma`s letters were published, florid tributes from Frederick were taken as retrospective proof that Hamilton had permitted his wife to accommodate the Bishop of Derry as well as the Hero of the Nile.

'Oh Emma, who`d ever be wise,
If madness be loving of thee?'

It does seem like an odd thing for a bishop to write to his friend`s young wife, but not untypical of this particular prelate. He travelled to Naples later that year and became quite close to Emma, in a mutually self-serving relationship that never progressed beyond a shared bawdy temperament, a love of mischief and a taste for intrigue at the Neapolitan court. However, because of Frederick`s eccentricity and Emma`s background, people were prepared to believe anything of them.

Amy Lyon was the daughter of a Cheshire blacksmith who, by the time she was 15, had worked as a maidservant and an actress, before becoming a mistress to one Sir Harry Featherstonhaugh, from West Sussex. Charmingly, he brought her as a 'hostess' to a protracted stag party thrown for a friend at his estate, where one of her duties was to dance naked on the table of an evening, although doubtless she had other duties. She left the party attached to a member of parliament called Charles Francis Greville, who took her down to London. Whilst Greville was sitting for a portrait, she met the fashionable artist, George Romney. Romney became obsessed with the beautiful young woman who now called herself Emma Hart, painting many pictures of her, which made her popular in society. She thought Greville would marry her, but unbeknownst to her, he was running out of money and had decided to marry a rich young heiress. The problem was, he couldn`t have Emma anywhere near him whilst he was courting the heiress, so in 1786, he tricked her into embarking on what she thought would be a few months` holiday in Naples. There, who else was waiting for her but Greville`s uncle, a much older man called Sir William Hamilton, whose first wife had died four years previously. In exchange for this fascinating new acquisition, Hamilton settled his nephew`s debts. Emma was furious, but pragmatism soon got the better of sentiment and she began to enjoy life in her exotic new environment.

She wowed Hamilton`s friends – including his occasional visitor, his old school chum the Earl Bishop – with a form of mime that she invented, called 'Attitudes.' This was a polite way for a roomful of guests to admire a statuesque woman. Without any underwear, using only a loose-fitting garment and a handful of props, Emma would represent figures from antiquity, sometimes copying poses from famous artworks. A bit like charades, the guests would try to recognise each new character as she assumed it. However, Emma wasn`t just a pretty face; she was also witty, clever and a very fine singer. The deal with Greville had always been that after he was settled with his heiress, Hamilton would return Emma to him. In 1791, Hamilton brought Emma back to London alright, but to marry her. Now it was Greville`s turn to be furious. It might be remembered that at this time, Frederick tried to persuade Hamilton to visit him at Downhill.

As a society hostess in Naples, the now Lady Hamilton knew respectability for the first time in her life. In the mid 1790s, she was 30 years old and in her prime. She became very friendly with the Queen of Naples, Maria Carolina of Austria, who was a sister of Marie Antoinette. Maria Carolina wore the breeches in her relationship with the Neapolitan king, Ferdinand; someone had to, because he was famously stupid and indolent. One of his favourite pastimes was pretending to be a peasant, selling fish in the marketplace. In the early days of the French Revolution, Maria Carolina had admired some of its ideals, but after her sister was beheaded, became somewhat anti-French. She ruled Naples with an Englishman as her prime minister, Sir John Acton. At that time, the kingdom comprised the southern half of Italy, as well as Sicily. With a bit of help from Emma, Frederick fitted right in at the court, hob-nobbing to his heart`s content, and confirming in his own mind at least, his unique position as a top-level emissary and intelligencer.

The Hamiltons had no fewer than four houses at their disposal; the Palazzo Sessa, which was the embassy building in Naples itself; the Villa Angelica, on the slopes of Vesuvius; the Villa Emma on the Bay of Naples; and a casino near Caserta, the immense royal palace north of Naples. Emma threw a constant round of parties, one of which was attended by Prince Augustus, a son of King George III, whom it might be remembered had almost ended up in a duel with Jack Hervey, over the affections of Lady Hatton. The prince was a good-natured but empty-headed dolt who fancied himself a great singer and was anything but. However, because he was royalty, his delusion was indulged – by everyone except Frederick. When, during the concert phase of this particular party, the prince sang aloud with the invited talent, Frederick shouted, *'Pray cease, you have the ears of an ass!'* The prince sang even louder, at which Frederick declared, *'This may be very fine braying but it is intolerable singing!'*

Frederick lingered in Naples until the spring of 1795, then wandered off northwards again. He devoted a large portion of his time to accumulating artwork, which he stored in warehouses mostly at Rome, but also Florence and Leghorn, as the English called the Tuscan port of Livorno. French emigres were selling anything they could carry on the cheap and Frederick picked up quite a few bargains that way. A letter from Bologna reflects a wistful desire to visit Downhill, were it not for the French revolutionary armies standing in his way, but this must have been but a brief burst of homesickness, for he could have circumvented the war had he really wanted to, and in any case had taken a five-year lease on a villa, Il Boschetto, on the Via Strozzi in Florence. The summer of 1795 found him at Munich; he had left one beautiful adventuress behind in Naples and was about to fall head over heels for another.

The rise of Madame Ritz

Wilhelmine Encke was born in 1753, in the Prussian royal city of Potsdam, near Berlin. Her father was a musician in the service of *der alte Fritz* (Old Fritz), as his subjects called Frederick the Great, or Frederick II, the enlightened absolutist monarch who greatly strengthened his kingdom during the mid-18th century. At its peak, Prussia comprised much of what is now northern Germany and northern Poland, stretching east along the Baltic as far as modern-day Lithuania. The kingdom was a byword for military efficiency, but Old Fritz was also a highly cultured individual: an accomplished flautist, a lifelong correspondent of Voltaire, and a patron of the composer Bach and the philosopher Immanuel Kant. Religiously tolerant, he was also responsible for some great architecture, like his summer palace at Potsdam, Sanssouci. Quite probably homosexual, Old Fritz died childless in 1786.

His throne went to his nephew, Frederick William II, who inherited his uncle's taste for high culture, but none of his work ethic, let alone his military or political skills. Idle and pleasure-loving, his subjects nicknamed him *der Dicke Luderjahn* – the Fat Bastard. A patron of Mozart and Beethoven, he set about bankrupting the kingdom that his father had built up. At the age of 25, he had seduced the 16 year-old daughter of one of his father's court musicians, Wilhelmine Encke, whom he nicknamed 'Minchen.' Instead of causing a scandal, the relationship was encouraged by Old Fritz to keep his nephew under control and the couple had two children; a son who died young; and a daughter, Countess Mariana von der Mark, of whom her father was very fond, even above his other, legitimate children. So by the time she enters our story, Wilhelmine was in her early forties and had been a royal mistress for her entire adult life. In the 1780s, to give her a gloss of respectability, she had been married to a chamberlain, one Johann Rietz. She then styled herself Madame Ritz, but everyone knew that the marriage was a sham. Her lover, *der Dicke Luderjahn*, will henceforth be referred to as the Prussian king, to avoid confusing him with our hero's son, also Frederick William.

Wilhelmine was described as tremendously beautiful and so good-humoured, cultivated and intelligent that no man could resist her. Frederick certainly couldn't. When they met at Munich, she was travelling south with a very large entourage for a tour of Italy, and Frederick was moving north with his retinue, to spend a few months in Berlin. Like two great ships, the pair collided. Any physical ardour between Wilhelmine and the Prussian king had long since cooled and she had recently conducted a passionate affair with a young Irish nobleman, Lord Templetown, of Castle Upton in Templepatrick, County Antrim. Templetown was 15 years younger than Wilhelmine, so in his mid-twenties at this point, and had been madly in love with her. One version of their story has the Prussian king putting an end to the affair and banishing Templetown, to prevent the young buck from carrying his consort off to Ireland, which is rather endearing given that the king had two legal wives, at least two other 'official' mistresses and goodness knows how many unofficial ones.

Another version has Templetown finding Wilhelmine in bed with a commoner, giving her a terrible beating, and then being banished by the king. Either way, when she met Frederick at a concert in Munich, Wilhelmine was on the rebound. Her journey south was ostensibly for health reasons, but it had been ordered by the king to help her – and presumably, everyone else – to forget about Templetown. In a twist to the plot that simply couldn`t be made up, unbeknownst to either Frederick or Wilhelmine at the time, far away in Britain, young Frederick William Hervey was avidly courting Templetown`s little sister, a Miss Elizabeth Upton.

Wilhelmine was unlike any of Frederick`s other flirtations. His letters to her went far beyond the florid niceties directed at Emma Hamilton and, many years previously, Frideswide Mussenden. Mostly, he tried to cajole her into spending time with him, as a smitten lover would. He pleaded with her to forget her *'fichu Irlandais'* (damned Irishman) and replace him with a *'Saint Eveque'* (saintly bishop). His infatuation did not diminish his sense of humour.

As with Frederick`s other female dalliances, again there is the question of 'did they or didn`t they?' In this case, it hardly matters, because any man who goes about with a miniature portrait of a woman hanging around his neck – as Frederick did with Wilhelmine – is most definitely in love. The fact that Wilhelmine had both the ear and the purse of the Prussian king was no doubt an added aphrodisiac. Frederick had gatecrashed the Neapolitan court on

Emma Hamilton's arm, now he used his acquaintance with Wilhelmine to insert himself at Potsdam. It was almost as if he was making up for King George III's snub, by placing himself on the best terms with the rest of European royalty. Nonetheless, he was no more respectful behind the Prussian king's back, calling him *'a lump of inert matter,'* and referring to himself as 'little David' and the king 'Goliath' in a flattering comparison of their respective girths.

A typical letter from Frederick to Wilhelmine from this time portrays his heart as *'a vast castle where the finest rooms are yours and yours alone; every appartment furnished in your name, with your charming face, and decorated with your tender spirit.'* On the subject of vast castles, he offered her the use of both Downhill and Ballyscullion, and even Ickworth, although the latter was barely a hole in the ground. After Munich, Wilhelmine continued south and Frederick reached Berlin, where he even gained access to her apartments: *'I would have you know that I spent two thoroughly delightful hours this morning contemplating your elegant bed, where the only thing missing to make everything perfect was you sleeping in it.'* Nowadays, he might be called a stalker.

To Frederick's annoyance, Prussia had recently signed a neutrality agreement with revolutionary France. In a synthesis of his love for Wilhelmine and for freelance politicking, he hatched a plan to introduce her at the Neapolitan court, where, he fondly imagined, she would be a stellar success. Under his guidance, she would then communicate back to her Prussian king the anti-French sentiment prevalent in that part of Italy, allowing Frederick to broker an alliance. That would show the British establishment what a player he was! In March 1795, his daughter, Louisa, had married Robert Jenkinson, the future Lord Hawkesbury and future 2nd Earl of Liverpool (whose father, incidentally, violently opposed the marriage because of Frederick's reputation). Jenkinson was a member of parliament and would eventually be Foreign Secretary, then Britain's youngest Prime Minister, a record he still holds to this day. As he had done with Bess and the Devonshires, Frederick now bombarded his until now largely-ignored youngest daughter with letters detailing his grand European schemes, presuming that her husband would appreciate them.

There was only one problem. Madame Ritz was a commoner and the Queen of Naples did not receive commoners, so Frederick persuaded the Prussian king to title her Countess Lichtenau of Pyrmont. Wilhelmine was in Venice when she heard this good news and immediately styled herself thus, travelling in even more majestic fashion. Frederick now hurried south, so as he could show her off around Naples. Passing through Bologna, he was seen by Lady Webster whom, it might be remembered, was last encountered fleeing Florence, after rejecting the advances of Jack Hervey in her carriage: *'Lord Bristol with some wretched dependents came to my inn; he dined one day with me. He is a clever, bad man.'*

Frederick asked Lady Webster for a copy of a portrait she had commissioned of herself, but she refused. Rushing on south, he caught up with Wilhelmine and introduced her to Queen Maria Carolina in January 1796; Countess Lichtenau was indeed the resounding success he had hoped for. The pair were observed in Naples by a young English traveller, a friend of Sir Walter Scott`s called Morritt, from Rokeby, near Durham. He described Wilhelmine as:

'…a very pleasant lively woman, the innamorato people attribute to her is a curious one, viz. Lord Bristol the Bishop of Derry, with whom she is very intimate & travelled part of her tour. Now, as she is young & also rich, I think the affair may admit of doubt though as to my lord he is the strangest being ever made, & with all the vices and follies of youth, a drunkard and an Aetheist, though a Bishop, constantly talking blasphemy, or indecently at least, and at the same time very clever & with infinite wit, in short a true Hervey. As he courts every young & every old woman he knows, I suppose that in the case of Madame de Ritz he has his own consent.'

Another observer, one of Wilhelmine's entourage, held a similar view of Frederick: *'He was remarkable for a revolting combination of witty knowledge, pride, ostentation, contempt and irreligion.'*

Emma Hamilton and Wilhelmine Encke, perhaps because of their similar backgrounds, immediately became firm friends. Behind Frederick's back, his chaplain, Trefusis Lovell, also imagined himself a firm friend of the Prussian beauty and corresponded with her frequently, calling her his 'sister'. The former Madame Ritz certainly was irresistible to men of all ages and backgrounds.

Family fortunes

Frederick was unable to savour his Neapolitan triumph for very long. Less than a month after introducing Wilhelmine at the court, in February 1796, he learned that his son, Jack, had died at sea. It might be remembered that Jack had returned to the Navy after his diplomatic disaster in Florence. Just a year short of his fortieth birthday, he was reported to have succumbed to a cold, which may indeed have been the case, but that was also a euphemism employed when members of Jack's social class succumbed to venereal disease. Another version has him sleeping in a freshly-painted cabin and catching his death from the fumes. Frederick collapsed and fell gravely ill, as he tended to do upon hearing this sort of news. No matter how uncaring he could seem to friends and family members when they were alive, in his own way, he sometimes cared very deeply indeed. A bizarre episode now unfolded, recounted by Lady Webster:

'Ld. Bristol was there (at Naples) *dangerously ill. As soon as the physician declared him in danger he sent to Italinski* (an artist) *for my picture, adding that though he had refused him a copy, he could not deny a dying man anything. Italinski was embarrassed, but sent the picture. As soon as it came he had it placed on an easel at the foot of*

his bed, and round it large cires d'eglise (church candles), *and for aught I know to the contrary he may still be contemplating my phiz. What makes this freak the more strange is, that it is not from regard to me, as he scarcely knows me, and never manifested much liking to me; probably it reminds him of some woman he once loved, and whose image occupies his mind in his last moments.'*

Some thought that Lady Webster bore a resemblance to Bess; both women were pretty and feisty. But whoever Lady Webster reminded him of, the strange cure worked, for Frederick not only recovered but positively rebounded, with yet another impudent plan.

It might be remembered that Wilhelmine had a daughter, Countess Mariana von der Mark, who was now of marrying age. In a scheme worthy of some medieval monarch, Frederick now decided that his previously *'undutiful and ungrateful'* son, Frederick William, would take Mariana as his bride. With Jack gone, Frederick William was now the Bristol heir apparent and with an eye to her adoring bishop's fortune and what she imagined to be his enormous influence back in England, Wilhelmine enthusiastically agreed. Frederick, for his part, knew that Wilhelmine owed her wealth and influence to the Prussian king. News had reached Italy that he was ill, so Wilhelmine hastened north whilst Frederick, who was still a tad unsteady on his own feet, would follow as soon as he could. The pair agreed to meet again at Pyrmont in Germany, where the king could seek a cure, where Frederick William could travel to see his blushing fiancee, and where the deal could be cemented. Frederick now described the *'undutiful and ungrateful'* Frederick William to his future mother-in-law:

I have no hesitation in saying that you will be captivated and really enchanted by him. He is a perfect man of the world – versed in literature, conversant with politics; a handsome countenance, beautiful features, a striking face – natural eloquence – charming manner, English modesty and reserve; with a pride worthy of his father and forebears... in the meantime, I should like you to write from Venice to Graft, the Dresden painter, telling him to go at once to Berlin and there paint a full-length portrait of your daughter. Let her be standing, wearing a perfect informal dress and above all nothing on her head – let her elbow be leaning on a very beautiful chimney-piece as if she were speaking to someone. In that way we shall have her expression, her face, her figure, her carriage and all that is necessary for considering her at her leisure.'

He certainly had it all figured out. By August, Frederick, Wilhelmine, Mariana and the ailing king were duly assembled at Pyrmont. However, as was so often the case with his children, Frederick failed to factor in what they themselves wanted. Frederick William, it might be remembered, had been courting an Irish girl called Elizabeth Upton, the sister of Wilhelmine's former beau, Lord Templetown. He truly loved her and refused to travel to Pyrmont. In exasperated disbelief, Frederick tried to drum Bess into his service, for some reason believing that she could persuade Frederick William to marry Mariana.

'I must confess it would half break my heart to see his fixed on any other than the beautiful, elegant, important and interesting object I have proposed to him. At least, dearest Eliza, if you have any interest with him, induce him, beg him, my dear, not to decide before he is able to choose. She would bring into our family £5,000 a year, besides a principality in Germany, an English Dukedom for Frederick or me, which the King of Prussia is determined to obtain in case the marriage takes place.'

Frederick also expected to be appointed, at the king's insistence, British envoy to Berlin and the union would even make the Herveys loosely related to the British royal family, for the Prussian king's eldest legitimate daughter was married to George III's second son. No wonder Frederick wanted it so badly. In one swoop, he could repair all the damage done by his antics with the Volunteers and return, triumphant, to the bosom of the British establishment. The proposal was as much about advancing his own interests, as his son's. Weeks slid by and his letters to Bess became more frantic. Next, the king was offering £100,000 as a dowry, which was an astronomical figure, akin to £16 million today. Elizabeth Upton, on the other hand, was *'a lady without fortune, without connexions.'* Frederick William faced a future of *'poverty, famine, and omnipotent love for her & her children,'* and if he died, she would be left a widow with orphans! The Prussian king had even promised to spend a summer at Ickworth if the wars with France ended, if Frederick could have his house ready, and if Frederick William would marry Mariana (and, one feels like adding, if pigs would fly).

And so he raved on, calling Bess a *'nasty little imp of silence'* when she did not answer his letters, then wondering whether she was *'alive or dead, or… on a journey?'* Summer turned to autumn at Pyrmont and still no sign of Frederick William. Back in England, Bess did not lift a finger to persuade him; too much water had passed under the Hervey family bridge for his grown-up children to be jumping at their father's beck and call. Frederick William was now 27 years old and had a mind of his own. Also, Frederick did not seem to grasp that his treatment of their mother might have soured his children against him. Even the normally-loyal Mary had grown to detest the way Elizabeth suffered in silent dignity, deprived of a decent income, whilst Frederick blew incredible sums of money on his whims.

Lastly, Bess had her own issues to be dealing with. Georgiana Devonshire had been very ill that year, struck down by a horrible infection that had caused one eye to swell to the size of a fist; she had been more needy of Bess than ever. Bess's estranged husband, John Foster – the former *Little f* – was also in poor health and indeed would die that autumn, allowing her, for the first time since her separation fifteen years previously, to become a mother to her two boys again. She also by now had two illegitimate children by the Duke of Devonshire; as well as Caro, she had borne him a son in 1788, once again travelling abroad to conceal the pregnancy and birth from Georgiana. One could say that Bess had enough on her plate without taking her younger brother to task over a proposal that he clearly had no interest in. By mid-September, Wilhelmine, Mariana and the king had left for Berlin, leaving Frederick at Pyrmont, still writing fruitless letters to Bess. Within a year, Mariana would marry one Count Frederick von Stolberg, in an unhappy union that would last two years, within which time Frederick William would marry his true love, Elizabeth Upton, in a faithful and happy union that would endure until her death almost half a century (and nine children) later.

The fall of Madame Ritz

During the past few years, the French revolutionary armies had invaded Spain, Germany, Austria and northern Italy (where their commander was Napoleon Bonaparte). Whilst attempting to muster Bess in his private campaign, Frederick also brought her up to date on the *'blackguard, pilfering, plundering, pillaging Republicans.'* After one of their defeats, he recounted how *'these ourang-cutangs* [sic] *ran without shoes, stockings, or breeches, and the exasperated peasants knocking them down, like real monkies, with bludgeons, pitchforks, staves, all that came to hand.'* However, French defeats were rare enough and the *'monkies'* would soon come to overshadow Frederick`s existence in ways that he perhaps should have foreseen, but did not. He followed Wilhelmine on to Berlin and the king even loaned him the enchanting palace of Sanssouci for a month or so, but sensing that he was no longer as welcome at the Prussian court as he previously had been, once again Frederick started south for Naples. His chaplain, Lovell, sent whining letters to Wilhelmine behind his back, complaining of his master`s pettiness, which if nothing else, showed a certain lack of self-awareness on his part.

By March 1797, the party had reached Trieste, where Frederick began to hatch his most impudent plan yet – a trip to Egypt. Even today, the south-eastern corner of the Mediterranean is a distant enough spot for the average European to travel to. In the 18th century, getting there was a huge undertaking, but Frederick was not proposing any half measures. Two boats, packed with artists, aristocrats, archaeologists and explorers, would make the journey up the Nile, where Frederick assured himself that obelisks and sphinxes could be purchased for the price of transporting them home. It is amusing to imagine the grounds of Ickworth, graced with sphinxes. Frederick even invited a young German naturalist called Alexander von Humboldt, who, on the basis that this strange old bishop was offering to pay all his expenses, agreed to go. However, the centrepiece of the expedition – the jewel of Frederick`s Nile, as it were – would be Wilhelmine herself.

Unfortunately, his jewel had absolutely no desire to make a lengthy and treacherous voyage into a strange land, whilst she was enjoying the elevated status that her new title gave her back at the Prussian court. Blue-blooded Germans still held her in contempt, but now that she was technically their equal, they attended her parties: '*the Countess appeared in a Grecian costume with a golden diadem in a mask… and sang after supper some lines composed by herself.*' She dabbled in politics and rarely left the ailing king`s side. Soon, she would wish herself in Egypt, but Frederick`s planning did not bear fruit. The relentless spread of the French across the Rhine and down through Italy made planning anything increasingly difficult and the following year, their most brilliant general, Napoleon Bonaparte, also decided on an Egyptian expedition, which put paid to Frederick`s idea, but perhaps goes to show that great egos often think alike.

On this occasion, Frederick did not even make it to his stated and more attainable destination of Naples. Instead, with no apparent aim in sight, he vented his restlessness on the Alps, criss-crossing them three times in sixteen months. He was in his late sixties and frequently unwell, yet increasingly unable to stay in one spot. He returned to Pyrmont in the summer of 1797, meeting Wilhelmine and the Prussian king again; *der Dicke Luderjahn* was on his last legs and Frederick wrote to William Hamilton in Naples, saying that the doctors wanted to send the monarch thence for a cure: '*if he has strength enough to reach it; your house would suit him well, & he might hire that, for he is antiquity mad, & bit by the same dog as you and I.'*

In their surreptitious letters to one another, Lovell and Wilhelmine called themselves Henry and Henrietta. Having gazed upon the irresistible Henrietta one last time, Lovell quit Frederick`s service and headed for home, after five years on the road; an incredible experience, seeing people and places that he would never have seen whilst languishing as a rector in Aghadowey, which even today is not exactly the centre of the known universe. However, he did not seem particularly grateful.

Then in November 1797, everything changed. The Prussian king finally died and was succeeded by his son (also Frederick William), a man as earnest and upright as his father had been decadent and debauched. Along with the rest of the court, the new king despised Wilhelmine and one of his very first acts was to have her thrown in prison, on two charges: collaborating with the English, and accepting bribes from the French. Frederick, who by now had returned to Trieste, wrote to William Hamilton:

'Poor Madame de Ritz is in Spandau (prison) *after playing the fool and some say the knave these last eleven months; she was arrested the day after the death of that old Porc d`Epicure.'*

Note the use of Wilhelmine`s common married name, rather than the title that Frederick had persuaded the late king to give her. If proof were ever needed that his passions could run cold as quickly as they boiled hot, it must be in this casual dismissal of the woman who had occupied all the rooms of his heart; the charming beauty he had paraded around Naples; his *'adorable Comtesse,'* to whom he had penned countless soppy letters. He was even partly responsible for one of her charges; believing Frederick to have the ear of British first minister Pitt the Younger, she had indeed collaborated with him! But Frederick was not prepared risk Spandau, by returning to Berlin to defend his former love.

Advance of the *monkies*

From Trieste, Frederick continued passing on news of French troop and ship movements to William Hamilton in Naples. If Wilhelmine's fate in the closing weeks of 1797 was a bad omen, then 1798 opened with another taste of what was to come. No army could long resist the French, but Frederick did not attribute this to any qualities on their part:

'Nothing can excede the venality of the Austrian officers except their lasciviousness, many of whom are in bed with their whores when they should have been in the field of Mars instead of Venus... I tremble for Naples once the monkies are able to reach Rome.'

The *monkies* had in fact reached Leghorn (Livorno), less than 180 miles from Rome, where it might be remembered that Frederick kept a warehouse stashed with artwork. His bankers there hired a ship to send this trove to Naples, to keep it out of French hands. Far from being pleased, Frederick was outraged; the cost of the transport was, he said, twice the value of the artwork. Since the cargo included paintings by Cimabue and his student Giotto, this might seem an extraordinary statement, for any work by these precursors of the Italian Renaissance would be priceless today. However, at the time, such 'primitive' masters could be picked up quite cheaply. It is not known what became of this shipment, except that it never was forwarded, like so many others beforehand, on to Ireland or indeed England.

Stories now accumulated of Frederick's growing eccentricity; when three of his fellow bishops wrote to him protesting at the length of time he was spending away from his diocese, he sent the head of the Church of Ireland, the Archbishop of Armagh, a blown-up bladder – like a leather balloon – into which he had inserted three peas. No explanation accompanied this unusual gift, other than a piece of verse signed *Bristol and Derry:*

'Three large blue-bottles sat upon three blown bladders;
Blow, bottle-flies, blow. Burst, blown bladders, burst.'

Frederick`s colleagues had a valid point, but it seems that by now, he really did not care what anyone thought of him. As the Italian dramatist Count Alfieri wrote to a friend: *'I forgot to say two words to you about that English bishop, Bristol. He is a madman, but not without ability or culture.'* At Siena, not far from Livorno, Frederick reportedly flung the steaming-hot contents of a pot of pasta out of his apartment window, onto a passing religious procession, because he could not stand the sound of its bells. Another version has him flinging the contents of his chamber pot. Either way, he was lucky to escape with his life; he fled through the rear of the building with his valet and bribed a nearby householder to conceal him from the enraged mob, which surely would have lynched him, with all the more enthusiasm when it was revealed that the blasphemer was a heretic bishop. Frederick waited until nightfall and escaped to Padua, then under the control of the French. He was barred from Tuscany, under pain of death.

As predicted, that February, the French did arrive in Rome, proclaimed it a republic and arrested the Pope (still Pius VI, although he died the following summer). Chaos ensued, and in the middle of it, Frederick`s main collection of artwork was impounded. Long believed to have been lost altogether, this was an extraordinary trove, priced by Frederick himself at £20,000, although the figure imparts no inkling of its modern value. Once again setting Bess an impossible task, he wrote to her, hoping to use the Devonshire`s influence to have himself appointed English ambassador to the new republic:

'I should save all that immense & valuable & beautiful property of large mosaick pavements, sumptuous chimney pieces for my new house, & pictures, statues, busts & marbles without end, first rate Titians & Raphaels, dear Guidos, and three old Caraccis – gran Dio che tesoro! (Great God, what treasure!)*'*

As well as his Titians and Raphaels, Frederick could also have mentioned paintings by Rubens, Caravaggio, Rembrandt and Tintoretto; the catalogue included nearly 600 items. However, if he knew that the French would reach Rome, why did he not take steps to have his trove moved? As already noted, the cost of ship hire may have been a factor, although this had never stopped him in the past. One letter to Harry Bruce in Ireland perhaps lends a clue; Frederick asked him to explore the possibility that the customs masters in Derry and Coleraine might allow him to land shiploads of artwork, passing the cargoes off as blank canvas and raw marble, to avoid paying duty. His extravagance abroad, as well as the cost of building Ickworth, often saw him short of money.

It has been alleged that he paid the French £10,000 to release his trove, only to have it confiscated again a week later. Whilst the figure seems improbably high, the trick was a common one. Over three hundred artists living in Rome signed a petition demanding the return of their great patron`s property, but that cut no ice either. Then, having impounded his treasure, the cursed *monkies* impounded Frederick himself.

Frederick the prisoner

Hoping to negotiate the release of artwork, in April 1798, Frederick travelled towards Rome from Venice, but fell ill near Bologna. En route, he had entertained French officers to dinner at an inn and pumped them about troop movements; certainly by this stage, since they controlled much of northern Italy, the French must have intercepted some of his letters and would have known about his amateur spying. He was arrested as he lay sick in a small village, but for all his talk of *monkies*, was treated kindly and not moved until he was able. Then, he was taken north to Milan and imprisoned in the Castello Sforzesco, which nowadays, ironically enough, is an art museum. Then, it was still a daunting fortress, but fortunately for

Frederick, his regime was not daunting in the least. We imagine prisoners hanging from chains in dank cells, but he had the use of an apartment, was allowed his own money, could order in his own food, write letters and even entertain guests. Indeed, the only drastic change to his lifestyle was being forced to remain in the same spot.

The ideals of the revolution which now detained our hero were about to wreak more havoc, in his adopted homeland of Ireland. Theobald Wolfe Tone was a young Protestant lawyer from Dublin; inspired by the French Revolution, he and a group of Belfast Volunteers had set up the Society of United Irishmen, which had seen some success in peacefully achieving Frederick`s old dream of Catholic emancipation (for example, the repeal of nearly all the Penal Laws). England made concessions, but for Tone and others, the reforms did not go far enough and partly at his persuasion, the French had moved to invade Ireland at the end of 1796. The very thing that the Volunteers had been set up to prevent, some of their number now helped to bring about. For England, it was the nightmare scenario of a foreign power kicking down its weak back door. Tone had convinced the French that the Irish would rise up and a force of 43 ships carrying 14,000 men sailed for Bantry Bay in Cork. However, a combination of bad weather and even worse organisation caused the French to turn back, when they were so close to the Irish shore that, according to Tone, he could have *'tossed a biscuit'* onto it. As part of the same plan, a much smaller French force actually did land near Fishguard in Wales, but it consisted mainly of mercenaries and was quickly defeated; to this day, the last foreign invasion of mainland Britain.

The British response in Ireland was to crack down with heavy repression, which partly caused the rebellion to kick off without French help in May 1798, just a few weeks after Frederick`s arrest. British troops were poured into the country and an estimated 10,000 people died in a series of battles, atrocities and reprisals (although some have put the figure as high as 50,000). Tone himself would be captured that autumn, trying to land with another, much smaller French force off Donegal. He would commit suicide before being executed and the British first minister, Pitt the Younger, would use the rebellion as an excuse to push through the Act of Union, abolishing the Irish parliament and merging the Kingdoms of Ireland and Great Britain, to form the United Kingdom (which, with one important modification, still stands to this day).

So in 1798, Frederick was probably safer in his Milanese prison, than he might have been in his Derry diocese. Not that the populace bore him any ill will, but Ireland was under harsh martial law and a noble birth was no longer any protection from British forces suppressing treasonable behaviour. After four months in the Castello, Frederick bribed the French governor of Milan, General Hullin, to let him go, but Hullin repeated the traditional trick of accepting the ransom and keeping the goods. Another story has Frederick bribing his guards but then refusing to escape and the guards being shot; this is sometimes muddled with yet another tale of him being smuggled out in a box and then betraying his co-conspirators. Both seem rather unlikely and at odds with the relaxed circumstances of his captivity.

What he did do at every opportunity was to invite French officers to his dining table, fill them full of wine and pump them for information; he subsequently maintained that many were disenchanted and willingly talked. It was equally possible that the French officers were deliberately spinning their feisty prisoner a web of disinformation and drinking his wine in sly amusement. Either way, not long after Frederick was finally released in February 1799, he wrote to the Hamiltons` new best friend, Horatio Nelson, detailing the intelligence he had gathered on the inside. Some people never learn, or maybe they just never give up. Specifically, he communicated that the major French military port of Toulon was in a rotten state and ready for the taking. Or perhaps, that was what the French wanted the British to believe. Later, he wrote another letter, this time to none other than Napoleon Bonaparte, to demand compensation for a gun that had been taken from him by his captors. It had cost 200 guineas (he claimed) and was being carried as a gift, probably for Ferdinand, the King of Naples, who was an enthusiastic huntsman (a hobby he shared with William Hamilton). Quite how these two great military geniuses reacted to Frederick`s missives, history unfortunately does not record. From the relative safety of Venice, he recommenced his intelligence updates to William Hamilton and also his abuse of the French; *'execrable highwaymen... a gang of thieves, pickpockets, cutthroats and cut-purses.'*

Happy Street

Frederick retraced his well-trodden steps up to Pyrmont during the summer of 1799, falling in along the way with a group of Breton nationalists. This prompted an exchange of letters with Louisa`s husband, now Lord Hawkesbury, about a proposal for England to invade France through Brittany. Hawkesbury was a boring but dependable sort and like a decent son-in-law, albeit one whom he had never met, sent courteous replies to Frederick, which gave every appearance of taking his schemes seriously. A few years later, as Foreign Secretary, Hawkesbury actually did ponder a scheme, previously suggested by Frederick, to partition France, but the concept did not pass the pondering stage.

Pyrmont must have seemed quite empty to Frederick without his old playmate Wilhelmine, who by this time was exiled to Glogow (in what is now Poland but was then part of Prussia). However, Pyrmont was not as desolate as the Naples he found, upon returning south again in the summer of 1800. The Hamiltons were gone and their charming residences were looted and half-ruined.

Whilst Frederick had been in jail, Nelson had destroyed Napoleon`s fleet in the Battle of the Nile. It was a bold victory and the British naval hero was celebrated wherever he went. The first place he went was Naples, where upon his arrival, Emma had thrown herself at him, crying *'Oh God, is it possible?'* She then threw him a 40th birthday party, inviting slightly under 2,000 guests. Tolerated and possibly even encouraged by her husband, Emma then threw herself on (the married) Nelson again and the pair embarked on a torrid affair. The maritime legend and his beautiful siren quickly became the most scandalously romantic couple of their day and quite possibly in British history. Next, Emma, William Hamilton and Queen Maria Carolina persuaded the lazy King Ferdinand to invade Rome; the hated French, it might be recalled, had occupied the Papal States and it was feared that Naples was next.

With the help of Nelson`s fleet, at first the invasion went well, but the French regrouped and sent the Neapolitans packing. Anarchy ensued; a civil war erupted in Naples and Nelson had to evacuate the royal family and the Hamiltons to Sicily. So Frederick arrived in Naples to find the British embassy, the Palazzo Sessa, partly demolished by a bomb, and the Villa Emma, the Hamiltons` seaside retreat, ransacked by a mob. How distant the elegant, carefree days must have seemed then. Frederick would never see Emma again, nor his old school chum.

More bad news was on the way. In December 1800, Elizabeth died at Ickworth from *'a violent spasm in the stomach. She was given brandy, but to no avail.'* A letter from Bess to one of her sons described her mother`s state of mind; *'We travelled rather with heavy hearts, for there had been unpleasant letters from my father, & my dear mother was low & unwell... most certainly he is a cruel man.'*

Frederick was now in Rome, but rather than falling ill, as he had done for Jack, Frideswide and even the Fighting Fitzgerald, he flew into a fenzy of letter-writing to Harry Bruce, about Elizabeth`s will. She had bequeathed some leases to be sold, which in Frederick`s opinion, were now his. Since onc lease was for the very land that Downhill stood on, he needed to prevent any sale. So Harry was ordered to ride pell-mell to Downhill and rummage through every drawer until he found the original leases.

As well as trying to resolve this crisis, increasingly frequent letters exhorted Harry to squeeze more money from rents and pathetically, Frederick once even tried to borrow £1,000 from Harry himself. His disorganised finances were the talk of society and are described here by Lord Cloncurry of Kildare, who came to Rome to get married:

'The noted Hervey, Earl of Bristol and Bishop of Derry… was in the habit of receiving regular remittances from home of upwards of £5,000 quarterly, which he immediately expended in the purchase of every article of vertu (artwork) *that came into his reach… wilful waste made woeful want and toward the end of the quarter the noble Prelate used to find his purse absolutely empty and his credit so low as to be insufficient to buy him a bottle of Orvieto* (wine). *There followed a dispersion of his collection as rapid as it was gathered, but as might be expected at a heavy discount.'*

In spite of, or perhaps because of the sequestration of his treasure trove, Frederick was obsessed with amassing another one, but still without making any practical arrangements to send his purchases home. The collector truly had overtaken the pragmatist. He saw himself as a latter-day Maecenas, the great art patron who had served under the Roman emperor, Octavian. No doubt, Rome`s artistic community flattered Frederick`s pretensions, but few outside such circles were happy with his spending habits. He fell out with his bankers, Messrs. Gosling and Sharpe of Fleet Street in London, who had the cheek to 'protest' the money he was drawing against them, then he tried to move his business over to Thomas Coutts & Co. He called Gosling and Sharpe 'madmen,' but as they were perfectly aware, Frederick`s English estates were entailed; they could not be sold, rather would pass to his heir Frederick William on his death. Only so much could be borrowed against them because any debt would also be carried over. As evidenced by Elizabeth`s will, the structure of his Irish property was downright insecure, since it depended on a hodgepodge of leases held by a variety of (not always trustworthy) trustees which also risked reverting to the church as they expired.

But Frederick was not about to modify his behaviour. He occupied a large house in Rome, which he shared with at least two artists and their wives, models, mistresses or whatever. Appropriately enough, the house was on 'Happy Street' or 'Lucky Street'; the Strada Felice, near the Trinita dei Monti, the Renaissance church at the top of the Spanish Steps. Strada Felice is now called the Via Sistina. He stopped giving any money to Mary and Bess; with typically acid wit, he now referred to his two eldest daughters as *'the widows.'* They in turn stopped writing to him, in protest over his parsimony and his behaviour towards their late mother. He stayed in touch with Louisa`s politically influential husband, Lord Hawkesbury, sending him sketches by Raphael. At a distance, he became reconciled to Frederick William. It would be nice to imagine that this was due to an ageing father regretting his treatment of his sensible and gentle son, but it probably had more to do with Frederick William obtaining the post of Under-Secretary for Foreign Affairs, where his boss was none other than Louisa`s husband. During a truce in the war with France, Frederick was hoping that Frederick William would intervene personally with Napoleon, over his confiscated treasure. In possible relation to this rapprochement, he drew up a new will, but it is not known how it differed from the 1791 testament that so damned his youngest son, for the document perished just before its author.

Bess did not bother with Frederick; she admired Napoleon and used the truce to visit Paris, where she attended a dinner given by the great political survivor, Talleyrand, and obtained a permit to go to Versailles. She found the great palace eerily boarded up, with grass growing in the courtyards, and portraits of the deposed royal family hidden in a lumber-room. She did not travel to Rome, but one of her sons, Augustus Foster, now a diplomat in his early twenties, visited his grandfather in the Strada Felice, where he found him *'surrounded by rascally servants and purchasing pictures by the dozen, some of them execrable.'* By now, his servants were mostly Italians, although Frederick referred to a groom called Henry, *'who quitted my service so abruptly, left a poor girl with child by him & fled the country to escape the Penalty.'* Another letter to Lord Hawkesbury foreshadowed what was to come;

'Thus far I had written when a most violent sudden unexpected & may I say unmerited fit of the gout – the most direful sugar-plumb of all Pandora's box – seized my chest & stomach with excruciating pains and perpetual vomiting which terminated in a delerium, and at last a total deprivation of sentiment & sensation.'

The airs of an Adonis

In 1802, Frederick suffered a fall from his horse, but he was not badly hurt and it shows that at the age of 72, he remained sprightly and active. He was still constantly on the move, although his enormous range had diminished; there were no more thousand-mile jaunts across the Alps and up to Pyrmont. Instead, he gravitated between Rome, Florence, Naples and their general surroundings. He kept his pen sharp, peppering his letters to Harry Bruce with amusing swipes at rectors, agents, attorneys and trustees, such as Sir Charles Davers, his late wife's brother: *'You must expect from him every possible infamous low-lived Blackguard trick that a Horse-jockey like him has been accustomed to practise for 30 years past.'* An agent called Gage *'sips whisky, gets his wife with Child, & never thinks.'* Another, Pat Brown, *'is a very honest but a very expensive, Ignorant, & presumptuous agent.'* A lawyer, James Galbraith, is *'a very blood sucker.'* A clergyman called McGhee is an *'Ingrained & thorough-paced sinner,'* whilst another rector, Soden, could be trusted *'with anything but one's purse & one's bottle… are my clergy mad & do gray hairs only bring on more expertness in fallacy & fraudulency?'* On the subject of his health, he sometimes shared too much information: *'My last Gout has cleansed the Augean Stable of my Bowels, & I am younger & stouter & more florid than ever, & ride 35 & 40 miles a day.'*

Whatever his flaws, Frederick's two most enduring qualities were his zest for life and his sense of humour, which are reflected in two snapshots from his final year. In the summer of 1802, in a letter to Lord Hawkesbury, he describes his idyllic routine at Castellammare di Stabia in the Bay of Naples, which has been a seaside resort since Roman times, and where he bathed to keep his gout away:

'Every being rises before the Sun, & away he marches with his desponding head & his staggering legs to drench his bowels with these acidulous waters. I take my dip in the balmy invigorating Sea-water – then to my ususal breakfast of delicious coffee blunted of all its irritating particles by the yellow of an egg instead of cream & with 2 fresh eggs warm from the nest to prey on instead of the coats of my stomach. Then after helping 'Hyperion to his Horse' I mount my horse & climb these beautiful mountains shaded by the broad leaved Chestnut tree for 3 hours regularly & then Home to a second breakfast copious as the first – yet such is the balmy aromatick salubrious quality of the atmosphere arising from various aromatick plants that it scarce supports the stomach until one o'clock – when all Castel a Mare rich & poor old & young native & foreigner sit down to dinner & to guess by the rest of my guests eat most voraciously in consequence of the vast space which the acidulated waters have left in Bowels & stomach – then succeeds a tribute to the warmth of the climate – a long sleep of at least 3 hours – then fresh exercise according to our various faculties. Few sup – I cannot fast till the morn – so a bottle of genuine Legitimate port wine with a few Potatos, at least as good & as mealy as your own Dutchy of Lancaster produces, supports my friend & me till the hour of Ten, when all Castel a Mare forget about their cares, diseases or medicine… such a life is worth at least a debate in either Houses of Parliament, & its pleasures surpass even that of a Majority.'

The reference to *'my friend'* is tantalising; was this friend male or female, and who were his voracious guests? He does not say, which leads one to suspect that they were not aristocratic and probably, not English (otherwise, he would have namedropped, as was his wont).

He had plenty of Italian acquaintances, but to what extent they were friends or hangers-on again is hard to say. When a lawyer called Colini asked to use his villa in Florence, Frederick granted him permission, but warned him that a Mrs. Wyndham might want it too; that he would have to let a Madame Fabroni and her family stay there the following October; and that he would need to come to some arrangement with a certain *chere Aspasie*, who was already living there and was to keep her rooms. Aspasie was described as *'l'amie de mon ame et de mon Coeur'* – 'the friend of my soul and of my Heart,' but Aspasie may not have been the tenant`s real name, rather a reference to the ancient Greek figure Aspasia, who was a beauty and an intellectual by some accounts, or a mistress and a brothel-keeper by others. With all these mystery women floating around, no wonder Colini wanted to live in the villa.

The second snapshot comes courtesy of a Miss Catherine Wilmot, in a letter to her brother, in the spring of 1803. Miss Wilmot was an Irishwoman from Drogheda, then travelling with a party led by Lord Mount Cashell of Galgorm Castle in County Antrim. Her hotel in Rome was in the same street as Frederick`s house, the Strada Felice, and although a prim, unmarried lady in her late twenties, she was an objective observer with neither axe to grind nor cause to flatter:

'As his house is an exhibition of the fine arts, we went to see it, and were amused as well with its contents, as the singularity of the arrangement. He is the patron of all modern artists, whose wives he not only associates with as his only female company, but has their pictures drawn as Venuses all over the House. His three favourite mistresses are beautifully represented as Juno, Minerva and Venus, in the Judgement of Paris. Tho` he is one of the greatest curiosities alive, yet such is his notorious character for profane conversation, & so great a reprobate is he, that the English do not esteem it a very creditable thing to be much in his society, excepting only where curiosity particularly prompts. I have often seen him riding & driving past our windows, & his appearance is so very singular that I must describe it to you. His figure is little, & his face very sharp & wicked;

on his head he wore a purple velvet night cap with a tassel of gold hanging over his shoulder & a sort of mitre to the front; silk stocking & slippers of the same colour, and a short round petticoat fringed with gold about his knees. A loose dressing gown of silk was then thrown over his shoulders. In this Merry Andrew trim he rode on horseback to the never-ending amusement of all beholders! The last time I saw him he was sitting in his carriage between two Italian women, dress'd in white Bed-gown & night-cap like a witch & giving himself the airs of an Adonis. The stories one hears of him are endless both in the line of immorality & irreligion, & in general he contrives to affront everyone he invites to his table. To counter-balance all this he admires the Arts, supports the Artists & spends such a quantity of money in Italy, that he has also purchased Friends. However his residence at Rome has thoroughly confirm'd the idea which most Foreigners have of the English character being the most bizarre in the world, bizarre but generous.'

Around the same time as Miss Wilmot was observing him from her window, Frederick described himself to Harry as *'in the greatest want of cash.'*

The end

Spring turned to summer, when wealthy Romans retreated to the cooler Albano area, south-east of the city. Frederick himself was fond of Lake Albano, overlooked by Castel Gandolfo, where he had holidayed with Elizabeth and little Louisa twenty-five years previously. On Friday the 8th of July 1803, he was travelling from Albano towards Rome in his coach, when he suffered an agonising attack of *'gout of the stomach.'*

There are two versions of what happened next; he was carried to a nearby house belonging to some peasants, who refused him a bed, because they did not want a heretic bishop to die under their roof. So

Frederick was consigned to their byre, to suffer in the stench. In the second version, his servants simply abandoned him screaming in his coach. It is possible that both versions are true and that Frederick`s servants ran away, before he was taken in by reluctant strangers, who heard his cries. In those days, travellers carried their important documents everywhere for safekeeping. As Nelson wrote afterwards to Emma Hamilton; *'He tore his last will a few hours before his death. It is said that it was giving everything to those Italian devils about him.'*

From letters kept in the Vatican archive, it appears that two of Frederick`s *'scoundrelly servants who spoiled their master in life and death,'* one Elia Giunti and one Guiseppe Vecchia, were sent to prison afterwards, but it is not clear why and they did not remain there for long. What can be said for certain is that Frederick died slowly, in great pain, with no comforts, friends or family, and most likely alone.

His death mass in Rome was attended by 800 mourners, most of them artists, but none of Frederick`s family travelled there, not even afterwards, to repatriate his remains, nor to deal with his affairs. Sealed in a lead coffin, his body stayed in Rome for quite some time, until from common decency, the new British envoy to Naples, Hamilton`s replacement, Hugh Elliot, arranged to send it back to England on a Royal Navy warship, the Monmouth. Because sailors were superstitious about having corpses on board, Frederick was packed in a crate marked 'antique statue,' which gave rise to the rather apt myth that his body had been lost and a statue buried in its place.

When Captain George Hart of the Monmouth arrived at Portsmouth, he found no-one waiting, so the coffin travelled on to London by post, as if Frederick were just a piece of art, furniture or some other souvenir, sent home from the continent. A few weeks later, Hart called to see the Herveys and Lord Hawkesbury, but *'none of Lord Bristol`s family has thought it necessary to take the smallest notice of* *me… it appears to me as if they were offended with me for bringing to England the remains of the late Earl of Bristol.'*

Nearly ten months after his death, on the 21st of April 1804, Frederick was finally laid to rest beside his brothers George and Augustus, in St Mary`s church in the grounds of Ickworth, where Hervey males have been buried since 1467.

Epilogue

The end of Frederick's story leaves so many others unfinished that it would take several more books to do them justice. In some cases, these have already been written, but it is worth summarising what befell the people most closely associated with him.

William and Emma Hamilton. Partly because of the fiasco in Naples and partly to force Nelson to come home, William Hamilton was recalled in 1800. The Hamiltons returned to London with Nelson, where they lived together in a menage that had all of Britain fascinated and scandalised. William died even before Frederick, in April 1803, and just over two years later, Nelson famously bowed out at Trafalgar. Emma had no children by William, but two daughters by Nelson; one died in infancy and the other, Horatia, grew up and married a clergyman, refusing to acknowledge Emma as her mother. In 1815, aged 50, Emma died; broken, alcoholic, overweight, in debt and in Calais, where she had fled to escape her creditors.

Bess and the Devonshires. Georgiana died in 1806, at which point the Duke discovered the true extent of her gambling debts. Apparently, she owed about £3 million in today's money and when informed of the sum, he reportedly asked, *'Is that all?'* Three years later, he married Bess, but passed away after only two years of wedded bliss. Bess maintained her talent for turning up in all the right places; she watched Napoleon parade in Paris and attended Nelson's funeral. After the Duke's death, she lived in Rome, where she led a very similar lifestyle to her father's, relishing the antiquities, the arts and her status as a social curiosity. She wrote seven novels, only one of which was published under her name and in her lifetime. She died in Rome in 1824, at the age of 66, again like her father, in quite a lot of debt.

Lady Erne. Frederick's oldest daughter, Mary, lived mainly in England after her father's death. She and Bess contested his will, the 1791 version, but nothing much came of that. Mary died at Hampton

Court Palace in 1842, at the age of 89. Her daughter Caroline, the little girl pictured with Frederick in the grounds of the Villa Borghese (see photographs), married a descendant of Lady Mary Wortley Montagu, who alongside Voltaire is considered the strongest claimant for coining the witticism that when God created the human race, he created men, women and Herveys.

Louisa and Lord Liverpool. Frederick`s youngest daughter became Lady Liverpool when her husband inerited his father`s title. As noted, Liverpool was Britain`s youngest prime minister, serving from 1812 to 1827. He was also considered one of the dullest, although he managed the country through the Napoleonic wars, a banking crisis, Catholic emancipation and the Peterloo Massacre. It was often said of Louisa that she was remarkably chaste and well-behaved for a Hervey, although she was neurotic in her own, quiet way. She spent much of her later life engaged in charitable works and died in 1821, at the age of 54. Liverpool remarried, but died in office seven years later.

Frederick William Hervey, the 5th Earl of Bristol. As Frederick`s heir, his youngest son`s story is linked to his father`s property. The Roman treasure trove, confiscated by the French, was reputed to have ended up in the Louvre in Paris, but Napoleon looted so many important art treasures from Rome that confusion was inevitable. Whilst fragments of it were no doubt snaffled by the French, the vast bulk was auctioned off in 1806 at the College of St Isidore in Rome, which appropriately enough, is an Irish College. Much of the proceeds and many of the actual items went to settle Frederick`s Roman creditors, not least his banker, one Giovanni Torlonia, who built the Villa Torlonia, which nowadays, of all things, is a museum with a small collection of classical statues. Whether any of these ever belonged to Frederick is hard to say; Benito Mussolini occupied the villa for a time and afterwards, it fell derelict for many decades. A shipload of items salvaged by Frederick William from the trove was supposedly wrecked, although it was alleged that the cargo was in fact stolen. Some of Ickworth`s chimneypieces did come from the trove; the fate of most of the items is currently unknown.

Frederick never saw the extraordinary house that he started at Ickworth. For many years after his death, only the shell of the rotunda stood, as Frederick William paid off some of his father`s debts, even taking his family abroad to live more cheaply. The price of agricultural land rocketed during the Napoleonic Wars and the Hervey fortune recovered; Frederick William completed his father`s mansion and occupied it in 1829. He lived to the age of 90, every inch the respectable country gent.

However, later generations went some way towards matching Frederick`s notoriety. Victor Hervey, the 6th Marquess of Bristol (1915-85), also known as 'the Reptile,' served a spell in jail for stealing jewellery. He was reputedly the inspiration for the original Pink Panther film, where David Niven plays an aristocratic jewel thief. His son, Frederick William John Augustus Hervey, the 7th Marquess (1954-1999), was a flamboyant homosexual who reputedly wasted £35 million, most of it on drugs and male prostitutes. Ickworth was handed to the National Trust in 1956, but part of the deal allowed male heirs to occupy the east wing on a 99-year lease. John sold the lease to the Trust in 1998 before dying of Aids. Ickworth House is a must-see destination for anyone interested in architecture, history or art. The east wing is now a hotel.

On the subject of hotels, a popular myth is that all over Europe, thanks to his fame as an upmarket traveller, hotels are called Bristol after Frederick. It has even been suggested that some assumed the title to attract his custom, but no-one can point to a Hotel Bristol that existed in his lifetime and most were built long after, when the railways opened up mass tourism. The Hotel Bristols in Rome and Vienna are christened after the city, not Frederick, and it seems that 'Bristol' is most likely a generic name, like 'Astoria,' or 'Ritz.'

Frederick is remembered in other ways. Visible to the west of Ickworth House is a large obelisk. In the 35 years that he was Bishop of Derry, Frederick spent less than 12 in his diocese, yet he was so fondly-regarded that after his death, Protestants, Presbyterians and Catholics came together to pay for this memorial. *'He was the friend and protector of them all,'* declares part of the lengthy dedication. Given the sectarian hatred that simmers in Ireland to this day, but which burned out of control when it was commissioned, this monument is a testament to Frederick's greatest legacy – his religious tolerance.

Madame Ritz. Napoleon conquered Prussia in 1806, defeating the regime that had exiled Wilhelmine. She immediately petitioned his Imperial and Royal Majesty, Emperor of the French, King of Italy and Protector of the Confederation of the Rhine (as the revolutionary hero now styled himself) for the return of her confiscated property. Napoleon could or would not grant this, but he did grant Wilhelmine a pension and in 1811, she travelled to Paris to thank him in person. She briefly married a guitar-strumming Austrian playwright called Franz Holbein, or 'Fontano,' lived in Berlin, became an ardent German nationalist and died at the age of 67.

Harry Bruce. Like Frederick William, as Frederick's Irish heir, Harry's story is bound up with his properties there. Because it was so unusual for a humble clergyman to inherit not just one, but two mansions, their costly contents and so much land, to keep up appearances, Harry was admitted to the nobility as a baronet, the lowest rank. He made Downhill his home, but still preached at his church in Tamlaghtfinlagan every Sunday, coming and going in a massive coach. He inherited some of Frederick's debts and had his work cut out securing Frederick's leases, which later in the 1800s, were permanently bought from the church. Harry never used Ballyscullion; its contents were moved to Downhill and in 1813, he dismantled it to avoid paying window tax. Bits and pieces of Ballyscullion survive in other buildings around Northern Ireland and a handsome Victorian-era house now occupies Frederick's verdant plain. Harry died in 1822, aged 70.

The Bruces of Downhill were a more prosaic breed than the Herveys and during the 19th century, much less religiously tolerant than Frederick had been. Downhill itself suffered a major fire in 1851, which seems to have started close to Frederick's former bedroom. The Bruces claimed otherwise, but it was most likely accidental. The house was badly damaged and although many of Frederick's paintings were saved, most of his statues and his elegant interiors were lost. Downhill stood as a semi-ruin for 20 years, until the 3rd Baronet restored it, in the character of a Victorian hunting lodge. As with so many other landed families, the Bruce fortunes dwindled and the house was emptied of its contents between the two world wars. Used as a barracks during World War II, Downhill was sold and quickly deteriorated. It was acquired by the National Trust in 1980 and the walls diminished but stabilised. Visitors today try to imagine the glory of times past; Downhill is a romantic ruin, if ever there was one.

The little temple perched on the cliff fared a bit better, because the Trust acquired it much earlier, in 1947. However, even rock erodes over time and although the cliff has been reinforced, at some stage in the future, the Mussenden Temple will have to be moved away from its dramatic precipice, or Northern Ireland could lose its best-loved and most iconic building. The temple receives thousands of visitors every year; its interior did not survive and the walls are bare brick, but it is nonetheless a popular venue for weddings and cultural events. Not long ago, I attended a concert there, where a handful of beautiful young women sang and played music from Frederick's era. As I watched and listened, I could not help feeling that the Earl Bishop would have approved.

Acknowledgements

This book is not intended as an academic work, so its many sources are not catalogued. However, the following authors deserve particular credit; William S. Childe-Pemberton, for his two-volume life of the Earl Bishop (1924); John R. Walsh, for his essay *'Le Bienfaiteur des Catholiques'* (1972); Brian Fothergill, for *The Mitred Earl* (1974); Nicola F. Figgis, for her essay on Frederick`s Roman property (1989); Terence Reeves-Smyth, for his exhaustive survey of Downhill (1992); Jan Eccles, for her *Downhill Scrapbook* (1996); Lucy Moore, for *Amphibious Thing,* her life of Lord Hervey (2000); Caroline Chapman, for *Elizabeth and Georgiana* (2002); and David Erskine, who edited Augustus Hervey`s Journal (2002).

For supplying and giving permission to use the cover and interior photographs, thanks to; The National Trust; The National Gallery of Ireland; The National Maritime Museum, Greenwich; and the Stiftung Preussische Schlosser und Garten Berlin – Brandenburg.

For their endless patience and unstinting help, thanks to; Neil Robinson and Kate Yates of the National Trust at Ickworth; Max Bryant and all his staff at the National Trust, North Coast section in Northern Ireland; Jim Chestnutt of the National Trust in Fermanagh; Peter McMullan, my colleague at the Northern Regional College; Mike Jones of the Castlerock Historical Society; Barbara Campbell; Catherine Watt; and Rebecca Margaret Ricardo Campion.

Most of all, thanks to my mother, Kay Atherton, and my stepfather, Dave Atherton, without whom this book would not have been possible.

'That wicked prelate.' King George III

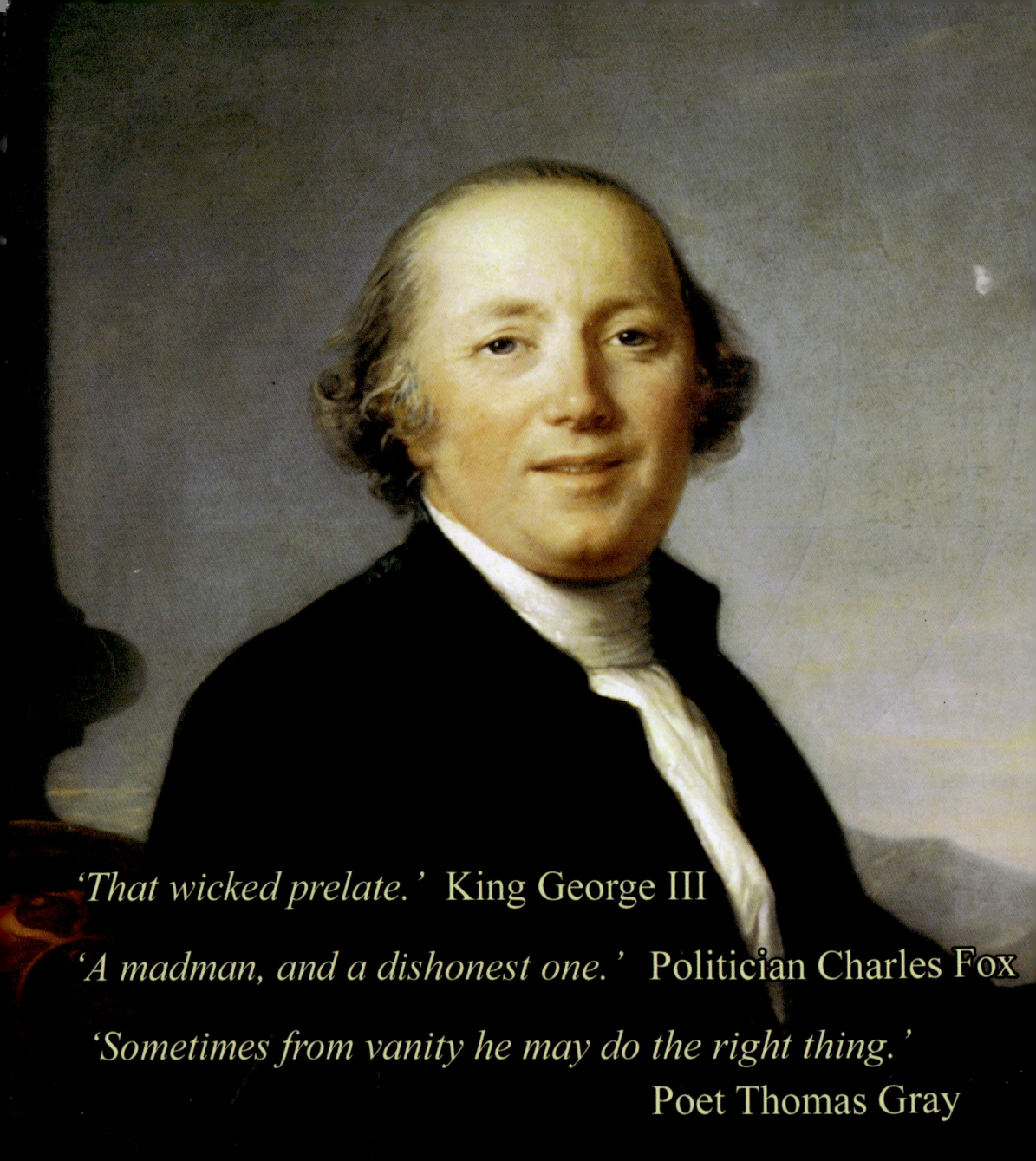

'A madman, and a dishonest one.' Politician Charles Fox

'Sometimes from vanity he may do the right thing.'
Poet Thomas Gray

It was the 18th century equivalent of winning the lottery. Through amazing luck, Frederick Hervey rose from obscurity to become a bishop and an earl. Although an Englishman, he became more Irish than the Irish; although a champion of tolerance, he spurned his family to collect art, mansions and beautiful women, to wander Europe and become a spy. This is his story.

GREAT
SEA

ISBN 978-0-9567993-0-2

£12.99